The advent, indeed the existence, of Southern Nationalism has long been at the core of an ongoing controversy among professional historians. Boyle provides a persuasive case for the dawning of that phenomenon during the early days of the American Republic in Georgetown and Horry Districts, South Carolina. The author demonstrates a keen sense of intimacy with the region and its people in his ability to capture a distinctly Southern point of view as gleaned from the proceedings of the local newspapers. The work is a gracefully condensed chronology of the road to disunion in which the author conveys the urgency of the Second Great Awakening and the Wilmot Proviso. In a country quickly changing in the Antebellum Era, Boyle explains how these events pushed the planters and yeoman alike further from the mainstream of American Society and into their own political milieu.

ROBERT T. OLIVER,
Senior Instructor of American History,
Coastal Carolina University

THE ROAD TO SECESSION IN ANTEBELLUM GEORGETOWN AND HORRY DISTRICTS

Christopher C. Boyle

FOREWORD BY J. BENJAMIN BURROUGHS

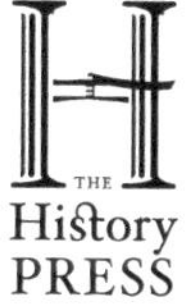

Published by The History Press
Charleston, SC
www.historypress.net

First published 2017

Manufactured in the United States

ISBN 9781467138987

Library of Congress Control Number: 2017947386

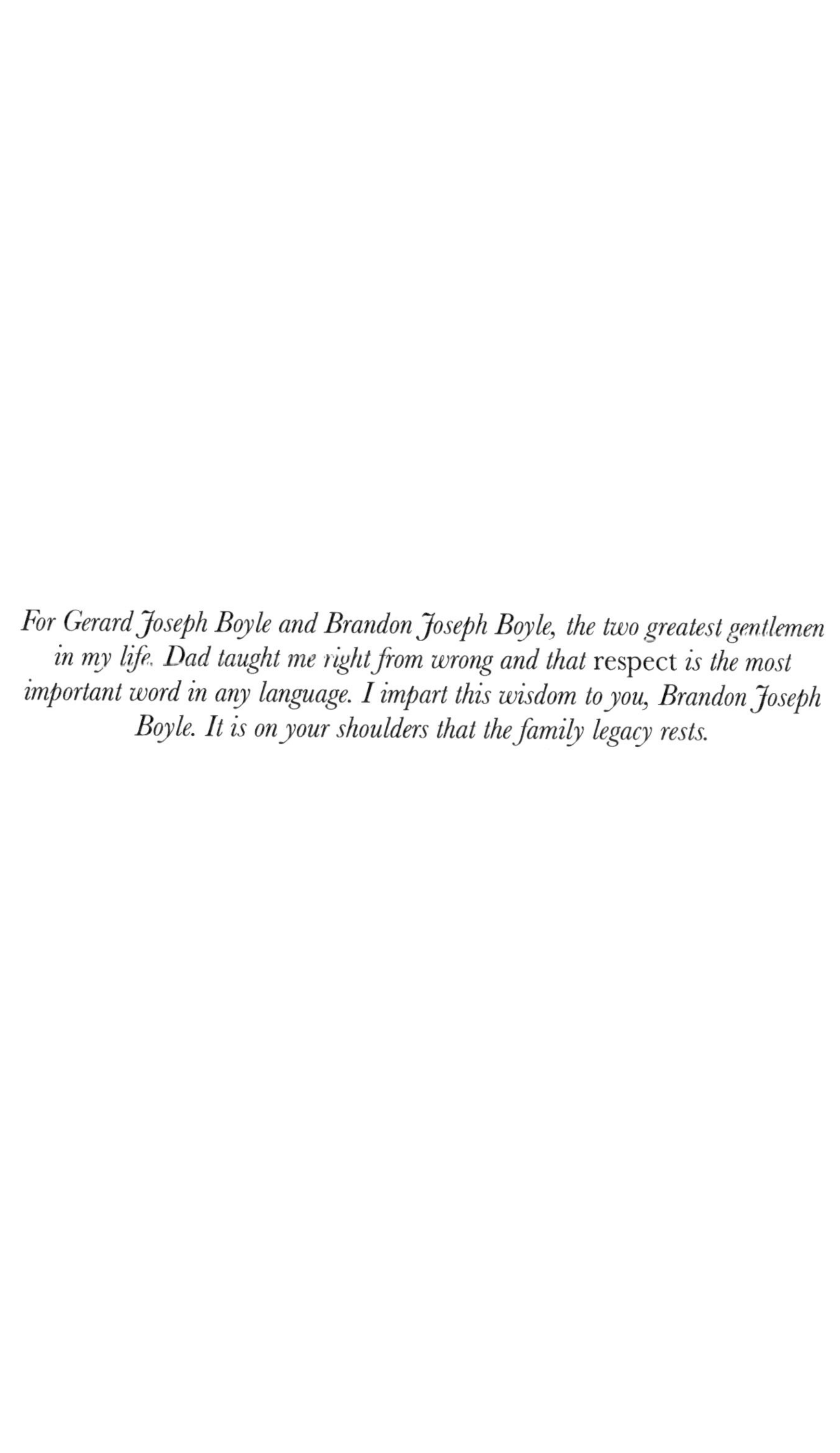

For Gerard Joseph Boyle and Brandon Joseph Boyle, the two greatest gentlemen in my life. Dad taught me right from wrong and that respect *is the most important word in any language. I impart this wisdom to you, Brandon Joseph Boyle. It is on your shoulders that the family legacy rests.*

Contents

FOREWORD

Georgetown and Horry Counties, located along the northeastern coastline of South Carolina, share an early history. This fact is often overlooked by many and explains why some do not fully understand the early political, social and family ties of the area. The land that was to become Georgetown and Horry Counties was once a part of a large coastal county known as Craven County. Craven County was established in 1682, and at first it only stretched north above Berkeley County (Charleston) to Winyah Bay. Later, it was extended to include a much larger area, including what was eventually to become all of Georgetown and Horry Counties. In 1769, the Georgetown Judicial District was created out of the old Craven County. That newly created district included land that would ultimately be divided into Georgetown, Horry, Williamsburg, Marion and Dillon Counties and a small part of Florence County.

In those early days, when Georgetown and Horry were first a part of Craven County, then part of Georgetown Judicial District and eventually separated into Georgetown and Horry Districts, the Anglican parishes in those areas served as political subdivisions. Those parishes were Prince George (1721), Prince Frederick (1734) and All Saints (1767). It was those historical parish lines that shaped the early history of this area, and it must be remembered that it was not until 1868 that the political election subdivisions as we know them today came into being for Georgetown and Horry Counties, eliminating the old parish system and thus the political ties between the two.

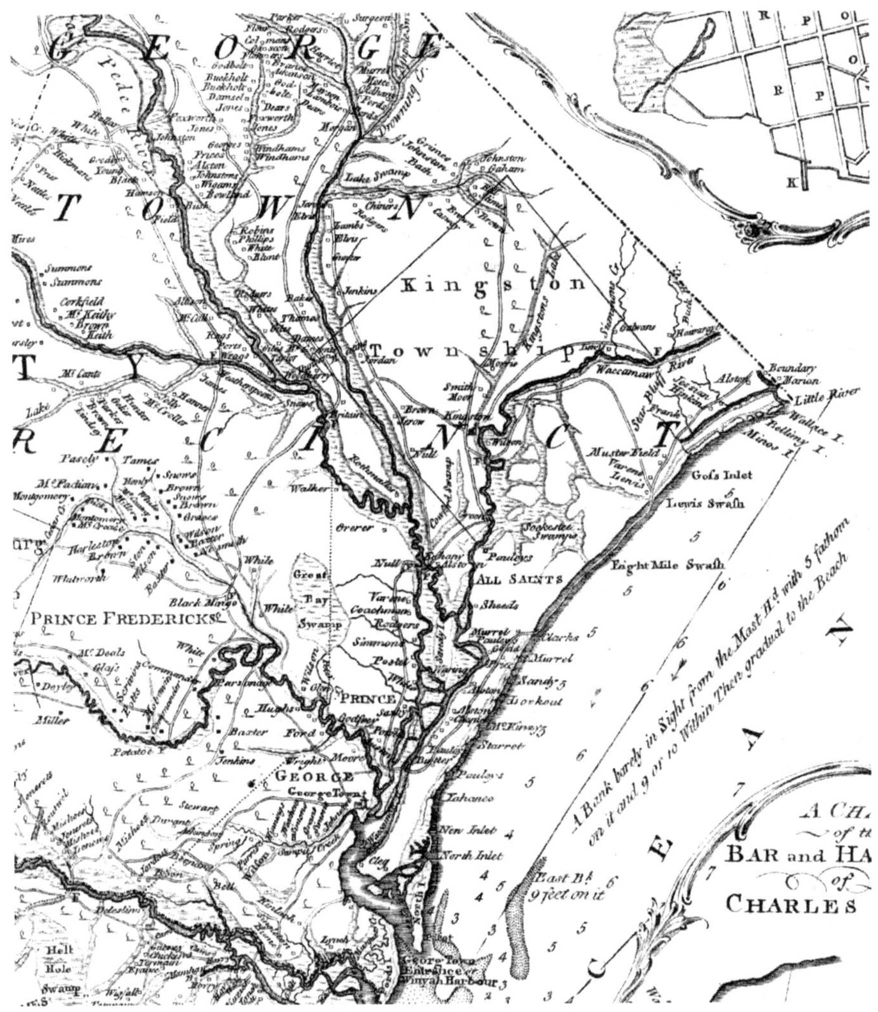

James Cook map of the Old Georgetown District, 1773. *Courtesy of the Horry County Archives.*

Early settlers to this area arrived in several different ways. Some came by ship directly into Winyah Bay, while others made their way up from the city of Charleston. Still others filtered down from Virginia and North Carolina, while some came by ship into the smaller inlets that dot the coastline of northeastern South Carolina. Whichever way they came to this area in the early days, once they settled on their land they would have looked to the town of Georgetown as the main community in the area regardless of how far upriver they lived, further uniting the inhabitants of the region. These settlers did not necessarily stay in one place once they got here. Oftentimes they moved around as the need required, relocating with ease across and along rivers, which in reality served as highways into the interior. It was not uncommon for family members to move from an area that would one day become Georgetown County to the area that would one day become Horry County—and vice versa. Thus, for those descending from the earliest settlers, a web of family connections was slowly spun over hundreds of years between these two areas, as well as with the rest of the old Georgetown District.

As is usually the case, the varying topography of the land dictated what types of agricultural products were best suited to be grown in any particular area. At first, there was not much difference in the types of crops grown or naval stores collected in these two coastal counties. However, eventually it would be realized that the tidal surge in the Lowcountry rivers lent itself to a new way of cultivating rice; that fact was responsible for the growth of wealthy family dynasties unmatched anywhere in the then young republic. While the wealth associated with the new rice dynasties created great differences in financial status in the region, many of the rice planters and yeoman farmers were still bound to one another in genealogical, communal and political ways. Those bonds were strengthened in the nineteenth century as outside political forces threatened to destroy their world.

In this book, *The Road to Secession in Antebellum Georgetown and Horry Districts*, Christopher C. Boyle examines those political forces and the motives behind them.

J. BENJAMIN BURROUGHS,
Horry County Historical Society

Preface

It can be said that I began writing this book in 1994 as part of my Old South history class at Winthrop University. At that time, I was writing a short history of the antebellum South Carolina rice culture. Part of the ten-page research paper included a couple of paragraphs detailing Georgetown and Horry Districts' reactions in regards to the events leading to the Civil War. Over the next two years, I continued to research the antebellum period and added to my collection of local reaction to the events leading to the American Civil War in my master's thesis: "Social Organizations and Leisurely Activities of the Georgetown Rice Planters, 1840–1861."

Years later, after publishing more than a dozen articles on local history, I published *Mansfield Plantation: A Legacy on the Black River* through The History Press in 2014. I borrowed my introduction and conclusion chapters, as well as my chronology of events leading to the war, from my thesis for my book on Mansfield Plantation. During the editorial phase of that work, I combined two chapters on antebellum politics into one and eliminated much of my chronology and local reaction to the coming of the Civil War from the manuscript.

After publishing *Mansfield Plantation: A Legacy on the Black River*, I began work on restructuring my master's thesis. As the work grew, I dove deeper into the causes of the American Civil War in order to better understand the planters' social organizations. My initial plan was to use my chronology as the introduction to the new book. As I wrote more and more about the coming of the Civil War, it became apparent that the book should be divided into two parts, with the first half of the reworked thesis serving as a study of the coming of war in Georgetown and Horry Districts.

By the time I was ready to publish the work, the manuscript was more than eighty-five thousand words. It became obvious to all parties involved with the publication (the Horry County Historical Society, the Winyah Indigo Society and The History Press) that the manuscript should be divided into two studies: one on the coming of the Civil War in Georgetown and Horry Districts and one on the social organizations of the Georgetown and Horry planters and their allies during the antebellum era.

Alas, my chronology of events leading to the American Civil War and reaction of the people of Georgetown and Horry has come to take on a life of its own. The study is no longer a support piece; the completed work now stands alone as an important study of the events leading to the war.

Acknowledgements

Many people deserve credit for assisting in the production of this book, as I have leaned on many people throughout the creation and editorial phases of this work. Mrs. Kelsy Kay Dailey served as my chief editor. She served as a grammarian and provided indispensable styling support to the manuscript. Without her assistance, I simply could not have completed this project.

My close personal friends J. Benjamin Burroughs, director of the Horry County Archives Center at Coastal Carolina University, and Robert T. Oliver, professor of history at Coastal Carolina University, provided me with an outlet for very serious historical discussions and helped to keep me focused on this project by challenging my knowledge of local history and pushing me to dig deeper into primary sources. Both of these gentlemen read the manuscript of this book prior to publication and offered several suggestions that prompted further research. For their assistance, all readers of this book are indebted.

Visuals for this work were provided by Horry County Archives, the South Caroliniana Library, University of South Carolina–Columbia, the Horry County Historical Society, South Carolina History and Archives and Mrs. Robert L. Lumpkin. My friends Paige Sawyer and Bob Howe each photographed for this project, and Rich Taylor assisted me in photo selection for this volume.

I would like to extend a warm debt of gratitude to thank the board of directors and members of the Horry County Historical Society who supported this endeavor. Besides reviewing the manuscript and offering insight into the project, Mr. J. Benjamin Burroughs contributed to this work by writing the foreword.

To my extended family, I thank you all for your patience and dedication. My siblings and their spouses—Ellen and Greg, Jerry and Roberta, Theresa and Bob—are all older than me and have always showed support for my endeavors. I would also like to thank their children and their spouses—Danny and Allison, Matthew and Deidra, Bobby, Shawn, Jerry, Erica, Andrew and Joseph—all of whom all bring me great joy and loving distraction from the tedium of research and writing. Also, to the start of the next generation of the extended Boyle family: bless you, Kayden.

To my parents, Jerry and Annette Boyle, how can I say enough? Thank you from the bottom of my heart for providing a loving environment for all of us that was instrumental to the development of all of our successful stories. Both of you have always been supportive throughout my education career and have always instilled in me the belief that I can succeed in anything I attempt as long as my heart is in the project.

I would also like to thank my little patchwork family for their support and toleration in listening to my stories of the past over the years of my research, as well as for helping divert my attention from my studies when I needed breaks. My beloved bride, D'Andrea Lynn, has taught me the true definition of devotion and love. My stepdaughter, Veda Kay Dailey; daughter, Hannah Grace; and son, Brandon Joseph, are each so different but collectively provide the spice of life to make our family complete. Lastly, I extend my appreciation to my beloved deceased son, Benjamin Charles. I thank you all for your gifts of love.

Introduction

The Rise of Southern Nationalism in Antebellum Georgetown and Horry Districts, South Carolina

Think back—often a retrospect delights the mind.
–Dante

Antebellum South Carolina was a state under siege, and Georgetown and Horry residents rallied the state against a triple threat from the North that endangered the South's traditional lifestyle. The growing tide of liberalism associated with the Second Great Awakening (an outpouring of social reforms that took place in the North and West), the growing industrial sector in the North that challenged the South's agricultural lifestyle and the federal government of the United States' willingness to change in order to accommodate the demands of the proponents of change prompted the people to react. In their newspapers, public lectures and groups, planters crafted a political alliance, unified themselves with the yeoman farmers and forged Southern Nationalism.

Rice planters and their allies were on the defensive during the antebellum era. Religious and social reformers criticized their lifestyle and their patriarchal code of chivalry as a medieval holdover of European tyranny. Agitators protested the planters' social, political and economic arrangement, first established on the North American continent in the Virginia Colony and inherited from the earliest settlers of Carolina, as oligarchical and promoting male-dominated authoritarianism. In short, the planter class, which had produced founding fathers and framers of the United States Constitution such as George Washington, Thomas Jefferson and James Madison, was accused of being barbaric and tyrannical.

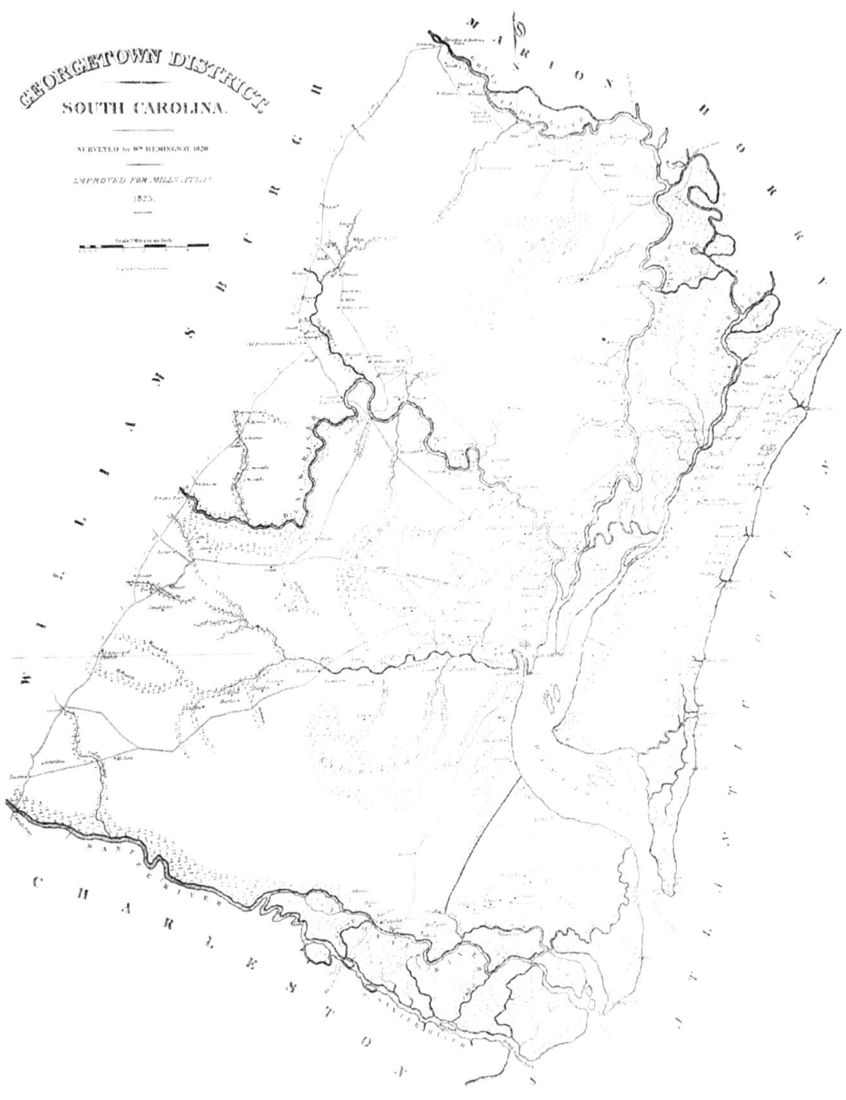

Georgetown District, 1825, by Robert Mills.

To planters, their lifestyle was not barbaric or tyrannical at all, but rather based on the founding principles of the United States. Like the founding fathers at the Continental Congress, rice planters held in esteem the enlightened argument put forth by English philosopher John Locke—the rights of life, liberty and property.

Planters agreed with the social contract that man creates governments to serve and protect himself and that if government fails to deliver basic rights (in this case, derived from God and defined by the government's founders) to citizens, in the words of Thomas Jefferson's Declaration of Independence, the people have "the right to alter or to abolish it, and to institute new government, laying its foundation on such principles, and organizing its powers in such form, as to them shall seem most likely to affect their safety and happiness."

The great southern agriculturalists clung to the American Revolution–era idea, passed down to them by their fathers, that local autonomy was better than a strong, central authority. They held fast to the ideas of the framers of the United States Constitution and the Bill of Rights that the Constitution was a governing document that set forth limitations on the central authority. They cherished the Tenth Amendment, which clearly stated that the powers not delegated to the United States by the Constitution, nor prohibited by the states, were reserved to the states or, respectively, to the people.

Many of the great planters of the era attended university in the northern states, where the Second Great Awakening was clearly visible, and in Europe, where the French Revolution had sown the seeds of change throughout the continent. They were exposed to the reforms underway; however, when the cavaliers of the Lowcountry returned home to their plantations, they quickly resumed their southern mindset of master and slave, along with their feudal, chivalrous code of ethics championing knights and ladies fair.

Thus, the formation of South Carolina College in 1805 signaled that South Carolina would educate its own sons. Fittingly, education began the task of unifying the Lowcountry planters with the upcountry farmers within the walls of South Carolina College.

One antebellum planter explained the Georgetown and Horry planters in the following manner: "The rice planters of the Black, Pee Dee, Samput [*sic*], Waccamaw and Santee Rivers were gentlemen of culture, educated at northern colleges or in Europe, who rarely sought the high and remunerative offices, but accepted without reluctance local appointments as school, charity, and road commissioners, and were ready to represent their district in the State legislature."[1]

The Lowcountry rice planters of antebellum South Carolina were captains of agriculture in a time when industry was in its infancy and husbandry dominated the economic, political and social structure of the South. They revolutionized the international rice market by empowering new industrial tools such as steam-powered threshing and pounding mills.

They continuously reinvested their profits into more land and slaves, resulting in large agriculturalists buying out smaller planters and becoming masters of multiple estates. With the smaller rice producers removed from the industry, larger planters were drawn closer socially and formed tighter political alliances.

From a twenty-first-century glance, it would appear that the professional and social positions of planters should have led to a stress-free existence. They had slaves to do the physically demanding work on their plantations and even kitchen staffs, maids, butlers, gardeners and coachmen to tend to their daily needs. The planter class enjoyed extended stays at the beach throughout the growing season, spent the holiday seasons at their plantations and enjoyed the social seasons in Charleston or took extensive vacations abroad. However, every highly effective aristocrat had to be a good businessman with enough aptitude, vigor and luck to stay ahead of the masses in a highly competitive and intensifying economic system.[2]

By the antebellum period (1820–60), planters had many professionals to lean on to help prepare and deliver their rice yields to market. They hired or promoted traveling overseers to serve as regional managers to watch over individual plantation overseers, who worked as production plant managers staffed by lower-level managers called drivers, who managed their plantation slaves. Some planters employed professional millers to prepare their harvests, factors to market their yields, shippers to move their produce to buyers around the world and bankers to handle their finances. With all of these professionals and laborers at their disposal, it would appear that the planter lifestyle was worry free and that their personal agricultural empires were self-sustaining.

However, this seemingly leisurely way of life, as touted by Hollywood and novels, oversimplifies the planter class and is far from the truth. In fact, the extended visits to the seaside resorts were necessary to escape the stagnant rice fields during the "sickly season." To remain on the plantations during the summer would almost certainly ensure that white southerners contracted "bilious fever," or "country fever," extreme cases of malaria.[3]

The social season in Charleston (between the Epiphany and Easter) was as much a business trip made for self-promotion and networking as it was for relaxation and withdrawal from the boredom of country living. There the planters attended balls and lavish parties. The social season ended with the jockey races.

At the top of the socioeconomic agricultural ladder, planters remained responsible for the work of their subordinates and the organization of the network that supported their trade. Like modern chief executive officers of Fortune 500 corporations with hundreds of employees, management staffs and various production sites, planters shouldered a tremendous burden in both managing their rice crops and regulating society norms.

The rice planters were successful businessmen who benefited financially from their occupation and place in society but stayed busy year-round by directing their plantations and civilization. Besides being agro-capitalists who adhered to Adam Smith's philosophy of laissez-faire free trade as described in his book *Wealth of Nations*, planters served their community, state and nation as politicians, agricultural scientists, physicians and civic leaders. They promoted education, internal improvements and the betterment of the general public. Collectively, the planter class held a great responsibility to maintain social order and to provide for their families, slaves and their less fortunate neighbors.

The Georgetown and Horry Districts comprised three parishes. Georgetown included Prince George Winyah Parish and lower All Saints Parish (a thin stretch of land bound by the Atlantic Ocean to the east and the Waccamaw River to the west), while Horry District included Kingston Parish and upper All Saints Parish.

Unlike the Georgetown rice planters—who dominated the economic, political and social atmosphere in their district—Horry District featured a more diverse economic group. The wealthiest among them were actually Georgetown rice planters, including Joshua John Ward, John D. Magill and Plowden C.J. Weston, who crossed the Georgetown border into Horry District to expand their rice planting empires. By 1850, Jacob Motte Alston had become the greatest rice planter in the Horry District. He had strong social and family ties to Georgetown but was a full-time member of Horry District. Unlike Georgetown planters who focused almost solely on the production of rice as a cash crop, Horry planters diversified their portfolios by harvesting sweet potatoes and corn as well. Peter Cox, Daniel W. Jordan, Thomas Randall, John Readmon, Peter Vaught, Daniel W. Oliver, Rueben George Weston Grissette, A.J. Graham, W.T. Anderson, John Lee and Margret Fowler all harvested rice in Horry on their plantations and farms.[4]

Another group of planters in the Horry District were those who operated pine plantations consisting of large acreages of longleaf pines. The pine planters harvested naval stores such as tar, pitch, turpentine and rosin from the pine trees and also sold timber for lumber. Pine planters of the 1850s included Benjamin Stevens, L. Thomas, John Thomas, Thomas Randall, Charles Walker, James Bellamy, William Suggs, Daniel W. Jordan, Peter

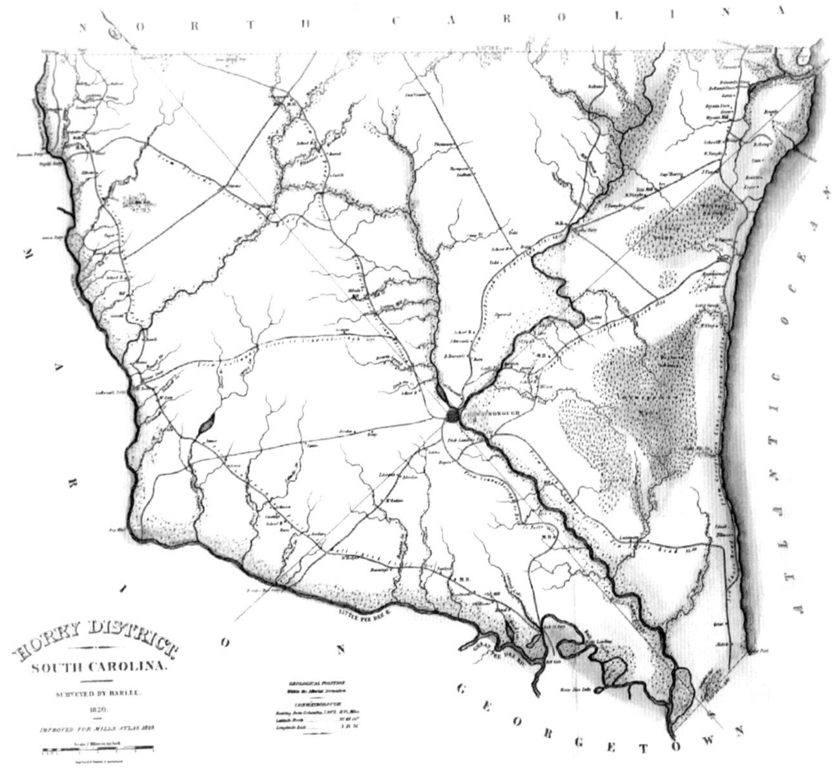

Horry District, 1825, by Robert Mills.

Cox, Thomas L. Hardee and Rubin Wallace. By 1850, Henry Buck had consolidated the Horry District's lumber industry by acquiring at least three steam-powered sawmills. William W. Shackelford was the only owner/operator of a steam-powered sawmill in Georgetown. Buck produced more than 900,000 feet of cypress, pine and hardwood lumber annually by 1850 and more than 4 million feet by 1860. By 1860, he had another milling operation in conjunction with Mr. Wright that produced 300,000 feet of lumber. In Georgetown, Shackelford produced 4 million feet of lumber in 1860. J.H. Riley competed with Shackelford for the Georgetown market. He produced 4 million feet of lumber in 1860 with the aid of a steam-powered mill as well.[5] It should be noted, however, that the majority of the lumber milled in Georgetown was harvested in Horry and floated downriver to Georgetown.[6]

Unlike the rice planters, who lived along the tidal-flooded rivers and the planters involved in the naval stores industry, who owned large tracts of the pine forests, the yeoman farmers lived on family-operated farms that they carved out of the pinelands. The yeoman farmers were hardy agrarians who tremendously outnumbered the minuscule (about 3 percent of the total population) planter elite. Simply put, the yeoman farmer was an average man who lived and worked on land that he owned alongside his family. His homestead was the most common economic, social and cultural locale in the Old South. These men had very limited resources, but they lived in a land of great white mobility and, like anyone else in a free economic society, dreamed of advancement. Like farmers everywhere in the United States, they were independent and proud.[7] The life of the yeomanry revolved around family and community. They did not vacation, but rather spent their social time helping neighboring farmers. Their social activities included corn husking, quilting bees, clearing fields, building barns and going to court to witness their government in action. For leisure, they rode horseback, participated in contests of speed and skills and competed for marksmanship with firearms. They bet on horseraces, cockfights and dogfights and played card games.[8] Like their husbands, the women worked hard, too. They cooked, sewed, washed, cleaned and bore and raised large families of children—around five on average and sometimes as many as ten or twelve.[9]

The yeoman followed politics and voted in large numbers. They were usually literate and enjoyed conversation and rhetoric. They reveled in the politics of the day, which always included all-day barbecues, long speeches and debates at rallies.[10] Without social media, musicians, sports stars or movie actors to emulate, the yeomanry looked to the planter class for role models. They aspired to become just like them, and even though social mobility to that level was impossible, they supported the system that the planters created because they knew that they had social status over the slaves and did not fill the lowest position in the social stratification of the South.

Although most yeoman farmers did not own slaves, the planters launched a huge public relations campaign to convince them that they had a vested interest in seeing slavery upheld. James DeBow published an article in his *DeBow's Review* magazine titled, "The Interest in Slavery of the Southern Non-Slaveholder," in which he gave several reasons as to why the yeoman class should fight to defend the delicate social structure of the South. He started by reminding the non-slaveholders that they received higher wages in the South than they would make in the northern factories, reinforcing the mindset that the yeoman farmers were above blacks in the southern caste system, and told them that since they were farmers they did not have to compete with European industrial workers, who lived in cities and worked with loud, dirty machines. He also reminded them that if they saved their money, they (or their children) could someday be able to buy their own slaves. Lastly, he reminded the yeomanry that they would all be overrun by freedmen if emancipation took place, and they would be forced to compete with the free blacks for jobs.[11] DeBow finished his essay with, "I think it but easy to show that the interest of the poorest non-slaveholder among us, is to make common cause with, and die in the last trenches in defense of, the slave property of his more favored neighbor."[12]

Contrary to New Englanders, who subscribed wholeheartedly to industrialization, southerners only utilized industrialization when it supported agriculture. Like cotton planters who accepted the cotton gin and cotton press to help them make agriculture more profitable, rice planters (such as Dr. Francis S. Parker) embraced the steam-powered rice threshing mill for removing chaff from rice. Other rice planters—such as James Heyward Trapier, Ralph I. Izard, William A. Alston, Joseph Blythe Allston, John Izard Middleton, John Hyrne Tucker, Joshua John Ward and Daniel W. Jordan—constructed steam-powered pounding mills for preparing the crops for market. Rice planters John Harleston Read Jr., Sextus T. Gaillard, Maurice Harvey Lance and Stephen Ford employed water-powered pounding mills on their plantations. As industry expanded throughout the United States, it began to challenge the supremacy of agriculture until the two ultimately became locked into a death struggle for omnipotence in the American Civil War.[13]

In that sense, the war that led to the fall of the planter class bears much greater significance than merely a contest to maintain slavery or even a challenge of the principles expounded in the United States Constitution. It was a contest between old world and new. A clash and struggle began between the traditions of millennia and a technological industrial sector that was barely one hundred years old at the time of conflict. It was the tried-and-true ways of living off the land versus the unsure and untested ways of modernity. At its epicenter was a question of identity. Southerners—planter and farmer alike—sought an answer to the lifelong question: where do I fit in in this new world order?

It was in the newspapers and public meetings addressed in this volume that Georgetown and Horry planters and yeoman farmers shared their ideas, argued their cases, discussed their options, forged Southern Nationalism and finally pledged their alliance to one another and their independence from the United States. Their grievances were not trivial, but rather monumental. They felt that their economic structure was challenged by their own central government, their social institutions threatened by their fellow citizens, and they had become politically neutralized as northern states swelled with immigrants and southern population showed little comparative growth. Southern rights had been trampled and their calls for redress denied. Lowcountry planters, and the entire American South, was faced with the age-old conundrum of standing up for their rights in a changing world or leaving the problem to their children's generation. In true paternalistic fashion, the men of the antebellum era, planter and farmer alike, shouldered the storm, unified and fought to defend their civilization.

Chapter 1

The Sons of Cavaliers and Puritans Form a Nation in the Western Hemisphere

A man's country is not a certain area of land, of mountains, rivers, and woods, but it is a principle; and patriotism is loyalty to that principle.
–George William Curtis

Division between the two regions of the United States was nothing new in 1860, nor was the call for secession. The differences between North and South were monumental, not trivial. It is far too simplistic to say that the war for southern independence was fought over the institution of slavery. The dissimilarity between the two distinct regions of the nation was steeped in differences in history, economics, religion and politics, as well as in widely differing geographies.

It is tragic how the sparring citizens of North and South could easily trace their roots to each other, having shared the struggles of the American Revolution and relished in its victory, as well as the victories of the War of 1812 and the Mexican-American War. From afar, the regions seem very similar in that they shared many of the same customs—Christianity, the English language, culture and history—but had distinctly different dreams for the future.

Geographically, the North and South are very different, and their differences dictated settlement patterns. The New England states have long, cold winters; thin, rocky soil; and rivers that do not run deep into the interior of the states but have excellent natural harbors. Consequently, northern producers of exportable products had to bring their goods to the coast in order to sell them, leading to the development of coastal towns.

The southern states, on the other hand, have navigable rivers that run far into their interiors. Ships could easily navigate up the South's river systems, enabling the purchase of produce and agricultural staples from Southerners at their own personal docks or landings and allowing for a rural life. The winters are mild, the soil is rich and rainfall is abundant. These basic geographical differences explain many things that influenced the division between North and South. Most importantly, they explain why New Englanders became fishermen and shippers and the South developed into a land of plantations and farms.

The Southern Colonies were originally set up for the development of plantations and were led by people who belonged to the Anglican Church and came to these shores to further their economic status. These members of the Church of England, descendants of the cavaliers of old, were the second or third sons of wealthy manor owners who, due to the English system of primogeniture, were not going to inherit their father's manor. Consequently, these privileged sons would not have the opportunity to become country gentlemen like their fathers. In an attempt to emulate the landed gentry of their fathers and older brothers, they came to America to set up plantations. Their counterparts to the north also came to America to seek economic profit as well, but (just as many Huguenots and Jewish people who came to Charles Town during the colonial period) also came to escape religious persecution and reform the Anglican Church. So, from the outset, the North and South were very different religiously.

However, while Englishmen came to the Southern Colonies to emulate their fathers' and brothers' country estates in England, England itself was in the midst of the greatest change in human history since the Neolithic Revolution. In the 1750s, England began the industrial revolution. The birth of industrialization had a profound impact on settlement patterns, occupations, pollution and social classes in England. People left the agricultural lifestyle in masses and headed to the population centers to labor in the new factories with their progressive idea of wage earning. Wage earning offered an almost immediate reward system for labors, as opposed to the agriculturists who toiled all year to sell their yields after harvest. Soon, crossroads became villages; villages grew into towns and towns swelled into cities as mills and mines sprung up throughout England. The wealth generated by industrialization allowed a new group of individuals to rise to prominence. The industrialist and his banker friends soon eclipsed the wealth and prestige of the great landowners and, in many instances, married into the old gentry to create a new ruling class in England. The old ways were fading in England, but in the American South, the agricultural tradition continued. Within a few decades, however, industrialization would spread to mainland Europe and to the northern section of the newly independent United States.

Based on these conditions, the North and South developed different political ideologies as well. During the 1770s, it was the New England colonies, descendants of Oliver Cromwell's Puritans of old, who found it easy to break with England since many had already broken with the king of England on religious principles before they arrived in America. For Southerners who belonged to the Anglican Church (most of the planters), King George III was accepted as their spiritual leader. To Southerners, the American Revolution had represented not only a political break from England but a religious break as well. After the American Revolution, members of the Anglican Church renamed their church the Episcopal Church, but the differences between North and South could not be so simply changed.

Even before the North and South agreed to come together to fight for independence from England, the two regions struggled over the question of slavery. Some colonial leaders believed that the institution was a stain on freedom and a symbol of European oppression that must be erased if the new nation was to be purified of England's subjugation. At the Second Continental Congress, John Adams, a Boston attorney, and Thomas Jefferson, a Virginia planter, proposed that the new nation ban slavery, but Edward Rutledge of South Carolina refused to concede. The entire South followed Rutledge's lead. Rutledge argued that the New England shippers made a considerable fortune in the triangular trade by bringing slaves from Africa to America and that the Boston shippers and merchants were just as guilty of offending God and humanity with the slave trade as the South was for holding slaves. He argued that northern shippers made their wealth from the trade and that southerners had the right to benefit from their investments. South Carolina and the other slaveholding southern states won the argument by threatening to refuse to sign the Declaration of Independence. The South got its way—the thirteen colonies united in mutual defense against England and achieved independence.

Fearing a strong centralized authority, the newly formed United States created the Articles of Confederation, a collection of strong states tied together by a weak central government. At first, the plan seemed well constructed to preserve local autonomy, but it quickly faltered. When delegates from the various states convened in Philadelphia in 1787 at a convention intended to "amend the Articles of Confederation," the delegates agreed that the central government was too weak to defend itself from internal and external strife and was not capable of growing strong due to its limited powers. Rather than "amend" the Articles of Confederation, the men (without prior state legislative approval) created a new government: the United States Constitution. While the various state representatives tried desperately to hammer out a new government that would suit all, northern politicians again attempted to remove slavery from the young nation. Southern delegates balked and refused to sign a document that would link them to a nation that would doom their economic well-being.

Politicians, states and regions made compromises in the creation of this new compact, the United States Constitution. Southerners agreed to end the international slave trade in 1808, twenty years after the Constitution would go into effect, and northerners agreed to give southern states representation for three out of five of their slaves in the House of Representatives. These actions, among others, enabled the states to stay together as one country.

Southerners agreed to the closing of the slave trade because they thought they had all the slaves they needed and that the region was on the verge of economic change. Three staple crops (rice, indigo and tobacco) had controlled the southern economy throughout its history from the settling of Jamestown, Virginia, to the 1790s, and two of them were faltering.

Indigo was only profitable during the colonial era because growers received a royal bounty for its production. With the loss of the royal subsidy on indigo at the onset of the American Revolution, the crop ceased to be profitable to export as the Spanish Guatemalan and French West Indian indigo crops dominated world markets. Tobacco, too, declined in importance as pipe smoking fell out of vogue in Europe. Of the original three staple crops, only rice remained important, and its production was restricted to tidally flooded areas and impounded coastal Carolina and Georgia swamps. Therefore, it appeared to southern planters that they had all the slaves they would need to conduct plantation business.

By the mid-1790s, the compromise to close the international slave trade had backfired on the South when the cotton gin and the rice threshing and pounding mills were invented. These inventions enabled planters to prepare more crops for market using mechanization. Suddenly, cotton production expanded throughout the South, and a large demand for workers ensued. With a limited supply of slaves due to the closure of trade, prices for slaves soared on the free market, resulting in larger investments for southern planters. Many Virginia and Maryland tobacco planters made their last big profits when they sold their laborers to the developing cotton kingdom.

George Washington was the first president of the United States under the new Constitution. Almost immediately, two political parties formed, pitting Alexander Hamilton, John Adams and their allies against Thomas Jefferson, James Madison and their allies. The main point of contention was the size of government. Hamilton, Adams and the Federalists believed in a loose interpretation of the Constitution whereby politicians had the authority to expand the power of the government as they interpreted the compact. Jefferson, Madison and the Democratic-Republicans believed that the only powers the federal government had were clearly expressed in the United States Constitution and that all other rights were reserved to the people and the states.

Fearful of a growing central authority under the administration of John Adams (second president of the United States), Vice President Thomas Jefferson and Virginia senator James Madison composed the Kentucky and Virginia Resolutions. The resolutions laid out the doctrine of states' rights and nullification. The authors argued that since the states created the United States Constitution, local governments had the authority to declare federal laws null and void within their states. From 1800 through the conclusion of the Civil War, the South clung to the ideals of Jefferson and Madison and was mostly a region of one political party.

During Thomas Jefferson's first presidential term, New England Federalists threatened secession from the Union. Unhappy that Jefferson made the Louisiana Purchase, which doubled the size of the Unites States, the Federalists complained that the president had rushed the purchase and that it provided more room for their enemies, the Democratic-Republicans, to expand their growing dominance in American politics. In 1807, seafaring New England again threatened secession when Jefferson passed the Embargo of 1807, which shut down all international American trade in an attempt to punish England and France (during the Napoleonic Wars) for seizing American freight and impressing American sailors.

During the War of 1812, South Carolina unified for war under governor and Georgetown rice planter Joseph Alston. The frontier West and plantation South were fused in the struggle to defeat England and its Native American allies, but not all Americans helped in the fight. New England shippers and merchants were guilty of active non-participation. The New England Federalists believed that England should be the ally of the United States and that the United States should make war on France instead. Both European parties were guilty of essentially the same offenses of stealing American freight, kidnapping American sailors and blocking Atlantic trade routes.

Since England's navy was dominant and committed many more offenses than France, and because the Democratic-Republicans traditionally favored an alliance with France, President James Madison declared war on England.

In late 1814, New England Federalist states sent delegates to meet in Hartford, Connecticut, to again discuss secession. The war ended before New England could declare its independence, and the convention proved the death knell to the Federalist Party, though not to its idea of strong central authority.

Chapter 2

Tariffs, Nullification and Southern Culture Under Assault

I think our government will remain virtuous for many centuries as long as they are chiefly agricultural; and this will be as long as there shall be vacant lands in any part of America. When they get piled upon one another in large cities as in Europe, they will become corrupt as in Europe.
—Thomas Jefferson to James Madison

The United States emerged from the War of 1812 unified under a banner of nationalism. For a short time, the nation was at political peace between the regions as shipping lanes were open to Europe, and southern agriculturalists willingly helped the young industrialist enterprises prosper. Although shipping was crippled during the war, New England industrialists benefited from the war economically by developing water-powered loom textile mills to process southern cotton. This new source of income became central to the division between North and South, as industry soon challenged agriculture's economic supremacy over the young republic.

Former president and ardent agriculturist Thomas Jefferson had spent his career encouraging the United States to remain tied to the land and prophesized that industrialization would pollute the landscape, create vast urban centers and eventually drive the United States into poverty. Nonetheless, northern states followed Alexander Hamilton's advice and industrialized. Soon, the United States became an empire unto itself and challenged the European masters for hegemony over the Western Hemisphere.

In 1816, during the "Era of Good Feelings," Kentucky senator Henry Clay proposed an act of three components called the American System.

The first dealt with a re-charter of the Federal Bank of the United States, which benefited all Americans. The other two components were designed to help the emerging New England manufacturing interests and the developing West.

The second component of the American System was the first tariff on imported goods in American history. A long-term goal of the Federalist Party, the tax raised the price of all goods entering the United States in an attempt to protect the struggling textile industry. By taxing imported goods, manufacturers could successfully compete with the cheaper English-made products. The move away from laissez-faire and toward government intervention in the economy would prove to be a major point of contention between the regions in the coming decades. The South agreed to a temporary 25 percent tariff on imports with the promise that it would be reduced to 20 percent by 1820.[14]

Immediately, English manufacturers adjusted the price of their mass-produced products by refusing to pay the market price for cotton and other raw materials, threatening to harvest the precious white fiber within their own empire in India and Egypt. Consequently, the American System caused readjustment in the international cotton market. As a result of the import tax, planters soon complained that tariffs were responsible for transferring the wealth of southern planters to the northern industrialists. Cotton planters lost profits, and citizens paid more for American-manufactured items, as imported goods, which had been historically cheaper, now cost more than the already expensive American-made products. In an attempt to promote and support industry, cheaper foreign-made products were no longer available and foreign products became synonymous with higher prices.

The third component of the American System arranged to help settlers reach newly opened western lands and help deliver products to market by creating internal improvements. The federal government funded these internal improvements from the money derived from the tariff on imported goods.

In summation, the American System was responsible for forcing the people of the South to accept less money for their raw materials while paying more for finished products. The North received the economic protection that allowed it to prosper, and the tax profits were used to develop the West.

Early in American history, the northern states dominated the House of Representatives due to their larger populations. Although the North dominated the lower branch of the legislature, four of the first five presidents of the country (representing thirty-two of the first thirty-six years of the

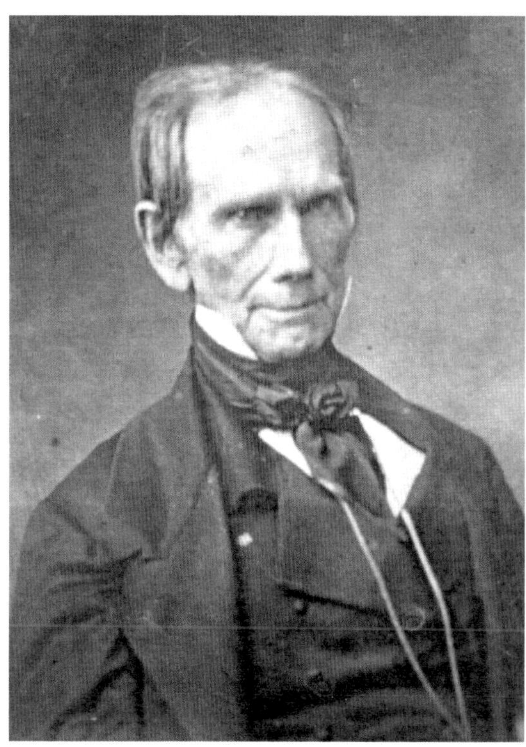

Henry Clay (Photographs Heyward Album). *Courtesy of the South Caroliniana Library, University of South Carolina, Columbia, South Carolina.*

United States under the Constitution) were planters, and southerners felt amply represented. However, by the mid-1820s, northerners and westerners began to dominate the executive office. The Senate held the only true balance of power between the regions, and the differences between the sections were further exacerbated by the complexities and political juggling associated with western expansion and the construction of internal improvements.

In the American System, the Senate voted on which roads, canals and bridges it felt most benefited the nation. The system set off sectional challenges between North and South to conquer the West and bring new states into the union that would vote for what best benefited their region, not necessarily the nation as a whole. The greatest internal improvement of the first half of the nineteenth century was the Erie Canal, which linked the Old Northwest to New York City. The construction of the canal, in conjunction with the opening of the New York Stock Exchange on Wall Street for business trading in 1817, made New York City the financial capital of the United States.

The question of Missouri statehood shattered the "Era of Good Feelings" and set off a further sectional dispute when the Senate refused to admit

Missouri to the United States because it had planned to become a slaveholding state. The admission of Missouri would have disrupted the Senate's balance of power between the "free" North and the slaveholding South. Senator Henry Clay came up with the Missouri Compromise to bring Missouri into the United States as a slaveholding state and Maine as a "free" state and divide the rest of the land acquired by the Louisiana Purchase along the thirty-six-latitude line. The balance in the Senate was maintained, and the nation's growth marched westward, bringing new states into the Union at an even rate to keep the delicate balance of power in the Senate.

In 1820, the previously promised tariff reduction from 25 percent to 20 percent did not take place. Instead, northern industrialists sought to increase the rate to provide further protection for their manufacturing interests. Drifting further from true laissez-faire capitalism and toward further federal government intervention in the economy, the government passed higher tariff laws in 1824 and 1828.

South Carolina governor and Georgetown lawyer and merchant John Lyde Wilson strongly opposed these tariffs. During Wilson's tenure as governor, Ohio suggested a national movement to emancipate all slaves. The federal government provided further slave agitation during Wilson's tenure as governor when it asked South Carolina to repeal the Seaman Act (an act that required all free blacks who were on trade ships that traded in South Carolina to be confined to stockades while the ship was in port following the Denmark Vesey slave insurrection). Wilson balked at both bills and remained stern in the face of northern and federal pressures.[15] The passage of tariffs and slavery agitation prompted Dr. Thomas Cooper, president of South Carolina College, to say, "It was time to calculate the value of the Union."[16]

The tariffs were a draw on southern wealth and essentially a bounty for northern industry. Tariff-driven sales swelled the coffers of manufacturers and also increased the already great economic distance between the northern capitalists and their wage-earning laborers.[17] The South protested that the North was buying the West's votes by providing its people with internal improvements funded by the tariff. Frustrated, South Carolina took the lead and declared John Quincy Adams's tariff of 1828 unconstitutional. The "Tariff of Abominations" imposed 45 percent taxes on certain items, and England again forced a readjustment to the world cotton market by decreasing the value of cotton from thirty-two cents per pound to eighteen.

In protest, United States Vice President John C. Calhoun published "South Carolina Exposition and Protest" anonymously to disguise his

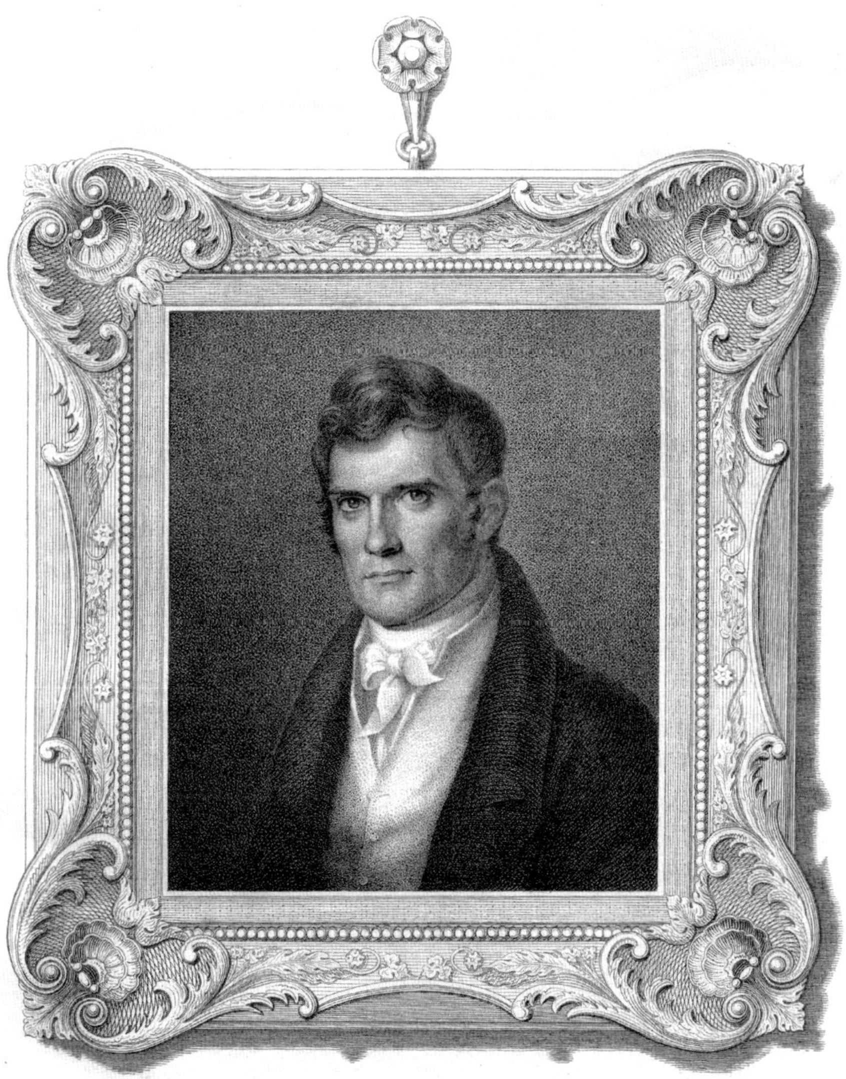

John C. Calhoun, engraved by J.B. Longacre after C.B. King; published by B.O. Tyler, Washington City (Prints Calhoun K-Z). *Courtesy of the South Caroliniana Library, University of South Carolina, Columbia, South Carolina.*

identity. South Carolina rallied to his call to nullify federal tax laws. Calhoun claimed that the states had a right, as described in Thomas Jefferson's and James Madison's Kentucky and Virginia Resolutions, to nullify federal laws that states deemed unconstitutional. Calhoun's argument became known as the Nullification Crisis.

In 1828, the nullifiers felt comforted when General Andrew Jackson was elected the next president of the United States. Jackson was born in South Carolina but came to fame as a westerner. Southerners thought that he would end the tariff; however, Jackson did not end the duty. He lowered the levy on many items to 35 percent, but South Carolina was not satisfied with the reduction and openly advocated secession.

In 1830, the situation intensified when President Andrew Jackson commissioned South Carolinian Joel Roberts Poinsett, the man who would eventually serve in various departments for five presidents (James Madison, James Monroe, John Quincy Adams, Andrew Jackson and Martin Van Buren) and spoke six languages (English, French, Spanish, Italian, German and Russian), and sent him to quell the perceived rebellion in South Carolina.[18] Poinsett served Jackson in Charleston by drumming up Union support, creating a pro-Union militia and equipping it with weapons to assist the landing of federal troops in the city and state in the event of insurrection.[19]

By the 1830s, South Carolina had become divided into three camps. One group, mostly slaveless upcountry farmers, were Union men who did not want to leave the safety of the United States. Two other groups were both secessionists. One group, the nullies, believed in immediate secession from the United States and promoted the idea of an independent nation of South Carolina if the other southern states would not secede with South Carolina. The other group, known as cooperationists, believed that South Carolina should wait on the other southern states to secede and form a Southern Confederacy.

In 1832, in reaction to the tariff and nullification controversy, Georgetown nullies formed the States' Rights and Free Trade Association.[20] The group held meetings throughout the year to discuss its options in the Union and if the time had come to act on secession. That year, Georgetown selected Thomas Pinckney Alston and four other Georgetonians to represent the district in the statewide States' Rights Convention in Charleston.[21] The assembly agreed that there was no hope for compromise in either branch of Congress since the legislature soon passed another tariff under Jackson.[22] South Carolina seemed destined to withdraw from the Union and civil war to break out. On November 6, 1832, U.S. Secretary of the Treasury Louis McLane sent letters to the tax collectors of Georgetown, Charleston and Beaufort explaining that South Carolina was in a state of upheaval and that it needed to be ready for any emergency. The letters reminded the tax collectors of their duties and powers as described in the 1799 "Act to Regulate the Collection of Duties on Imports and Tonnage."[23]

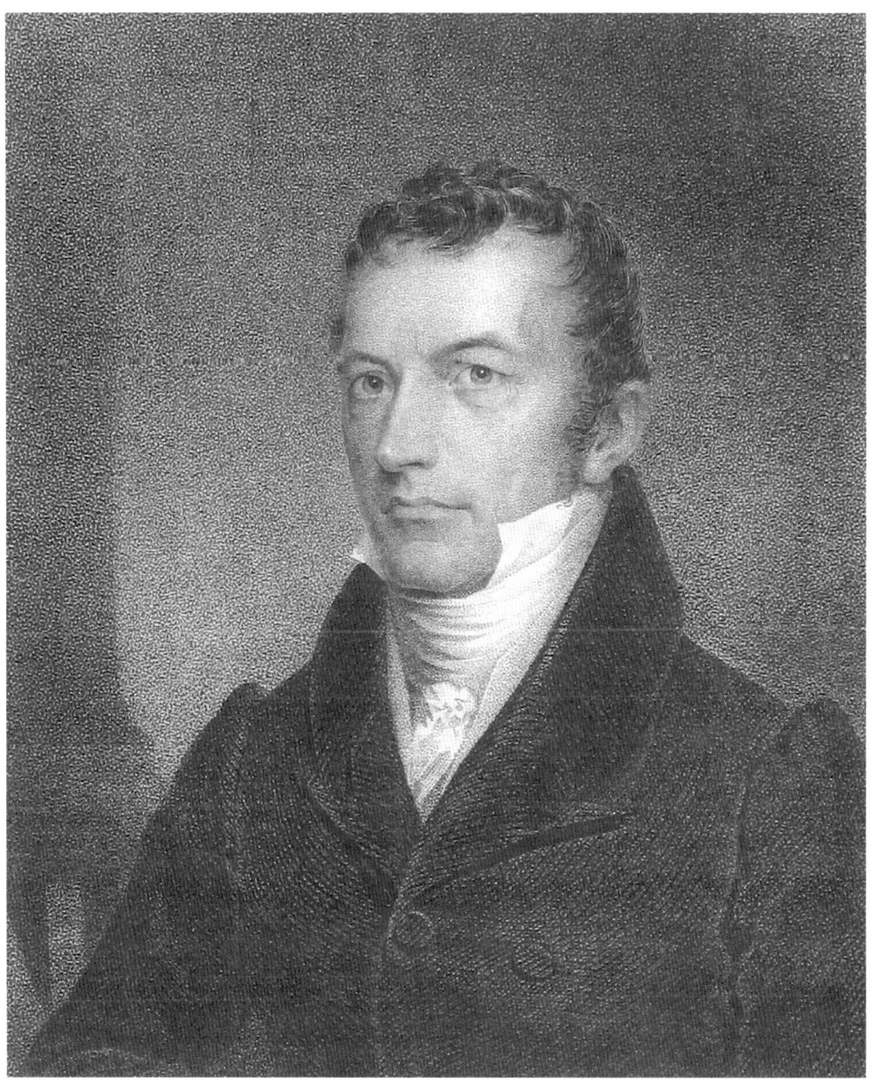

Joel R. Poinsett, engraved by J.B. Longacre (Prints Poinsett). *Courtesy of the South Caroliniana Library, University of South Carolina, Columbia, South Carolina.*

One month later, South Carolina senator Robert Y. Hayne resigned his Senate seat and took the position of governor. In his inaugural address, he said, "This is our own—our native land," and then told the people to "stand or fall with Carolina." He ordered $100,000 worth of weapons to defend the state and organized military forces.[24] Hayne chaired the convention that signed the Ordinance of Nullification, which declared the tariffs of

1828 and 1832 unconstitutional and, thereby, uncollectable in the state of South Carolina. The customhouse in Georgetown closed, along with many throughout the state. Militias began to drill in preparation for war.

The resistance to federal authority infuriated President Andrew Jackson. On March 1, 1833, Jackson opened the wound between the United States and South Carolina further when he passed the Force Bill, giving him legal authority to militarily force South Carolina to collect taxes for the federal government and to force the Palmetto State back into the Union if it seceded. With a pro-Union militia drilling under the aegis of one of its most celebrated and able politicians (Joel Roberts Poinsett), and with President Jackson's threats to send warships to bottle up its harbors and march five thousand troops to invade its soil, South Carolina stood on the cusp of destruction. Only a miracle could stave off open conflict and certain defeat.

Two weeks after the signing of the Force Bill, on March 15, 1833, Kentucky senator Henry Clay resolved the problem by pushing another act through congress. Clay proposed a compromise tariff that decreased the tariffs by 10 percent (1 percent per year) over the course of ten years but did not remove them entirely. The compromise pleased no one but avoided the ignition of open warfare. President Andrew Jackson recanted his pledge to send warships to blockade South Carolina's harbors and soldiers to invade the state. Later that month, nullifiers held a convention in Columbia to officially rescind the Ordinance of Nullification. Clay's compromise tariff disarmed both sides and temporarily avoided war.[25] Even after the nullification episode was over, as pertaining to the tariff, South Carolina maintained its militia of twenty thousand men. South Carolinians were determined to keep their freedom—even if they had to fight in its defense.[26]

Dr. George C. Rogers, in his book *The History of Georgetown County, South Carolina*, stated that the nullifiers of Georgetown acted toward the proclamation just as the people of Massachusetts had acted toward King George III during the coming of the American Revolution.[27] However, Georgetown was not yet united for secession, or even nullification of federal tax laws. Georgetown had two very politically driven newspapers during this period. The *Winyah Intelligencer*, which began publication in September 1817 and lasted until April 1835, was the newspaper of the States' Rights and Free Trade Association during the Nullification Crisis.[28] The nullies controlled All Saints Parish and attempted to expand their influence over the much larger and much more heavily populated Prince George Winyah Parish. The Georgetown unionists called All Saints Parish the "rotten borough" of Georgetown and Horry.[29]

When the *Winyah Intelligencer* wrote, "Any citizen appearing in arms against the State [South Carolina] would be guilty of treason," some pro-unionists threw bricks through the windows of the newspaper office and broke down the doors.[30] The unionists had their own paper in Georgetown. The *Georgetown Union* began publication in 1830 by John Matthews and Company, and later Taylor and Matthews, and ran until August 1839. The paper—which printed George Washington's famous quote, "United we stand—divided we fall" across the masthead—was the paper of the anti-nullifiers (moderate planters, immigrants, the town's middle class and northern-born men).[31]

The planters' complaints were not all political and economic. Besides being inherently different due to geographical influences and changes brought on by industrialization, many felt that social changes taking place in the northern states tore at the very fabric and societal structure of what their fathers and grandfathers fought for in the American Revolution. Two events, the French Revolution and the Second Great Awakening, were responsible for the changes challenging the South's traditional conservative social character.

The French Revolution changed Europe forever, and Napoleon Bonaparte's conquests and expansion throughout Europe in the early 1800s spread its ideals. The era of the French Revolution brought an end to slavery and monarchy in France (albeit revived for a short period after Napoleon's defeat) and ended the Catholic Church's control over France. It also brought forth the rise of nationalism, a national bank, state-funded and controlled schools and a uniformed code of laws known as the Napoleonic Code and witnessed women's calls for equality. In 1815, a European coalition defeated Napoleon, and the tide of his powerful army rolled back from the empires and territories that his armies conquered. The following year, the Congress of Vienna restored displaced monarchs to their thrones, but the fever of political and social revolutions could not be so easily subdued.

Like a virus spreading across the vast Atlantic Ocean, revolutions broke out throughout Latin America. Like Toussaint L'Ouverture, who led Haitian slaves in rebellion against their French owners, revolutionaries rose up against their colonial masters in the crumbling Latin and South American empires of Spain and Portugal. The successful independence movements prompted President James Monroe to issue the Monroe Doctrine to protect American interests from European recolonizing efforts.

In the United States, the social reforms of the French Revolution took root in Puritan-inspired New England's rocky soil and the growing cities of the Northeast. Immigrants fled the reemergence of the European monarchies and sought refuge for their liberal ideas in the Western Hemisphere. During the first half of the 1800s, the northern states were swept into a frenzy of change spawned by the French Revolution and the Second Great Awakening. The social modifications, however, conflicted with the traditional values and family structure of the planter class. Rice planters carefully created a world that centered on the Episcopal Church and lived by the propositions suggested in the *Winyah Observer* articles "Profanity—Don't Do It" and "Depend Upon Yourself and God Will Lead You," as well as articles on the Apostles and their wives and children.[32]

The Second Great Awakening saw the expansion of the Methodist and Baptist and, to a lesser extent, the Presbyterian sects among the farming and merchant classes through camp meeting revivals and evangelical circuit riders. The expansions of the Christian sects were not necessarily seen as threats by the planters, but the development of the Mormon religion (the Church of Jesus Christ of Latter-day Saints) was disdained. The Mormons boasted of ties to a lost tribe of Israel and claimed to possess another testament of the Bible. The *Winyah Observer* informed its readers that the origins of the "Book of Mormon" or "Golden Bible" and "its claim to a divine origin [are] wholly unfounded."[33] Later, the *Pee Dee Times* published an article titled, "An Illustration of Mormonism—the Truth Is Stranger than Fiction."[34]

Planters also eschewed the expansion of religious utopian communities such as the millennial optimistic Seventh-Day Adventist and Advent Christians, whose leaders prophesied the end of time and claimed to have mathematically figured out the return of Jesus Christ. They also questioned the beliefs of the Shakers, who alleged that all men and women were created equal and, as a result, banned sex (even for reproduction) because they claimed that sex was a tool that men used to dominate women. The Oneida community of upstate New York raised concerns among the planters due to their beliefs of complex marriage, sexual partner swapping and eugenic selection. These less developed Christian sects and communities offered new ideas that seemed outlandish and contrary to conservative Episcopal beliefs.

Adding to the religious deviations developing in the North and on the western frontier, deism and atheism rose. Thomas Paine's book *The Age of Reason* proposed that religion was created as a method to enslave the human race and that free people should break away from organized religion. Paine argued the deist principle that God created the universe and simply left the world and humans to their own devices, rendering religion and prayer useless. A group of anti-religious people in Boston, Massachusetts, held the Anti-Sabbath Convention. William Lloyd Garrison and Lucretia Mott led the convention and "spoke to a packed house and their message was very well received." They proposed that honoring Sunday as a holy day and a day of rest violated their First Amendment right of freedom of, and freedom from, religion. The convention, supported by industrialization, proposed that steamboats and railroad traffic commence on Sunday and that factories and businesses conduct trade as normal. Garrison went so far as to declare that "ministers are wolves in sheep clothing" and accused them of being "Christian Tyrants."[35]

At the same time of these religious upheavals and broadening of religious diversity in Christian sects and utopian communities, women reformers challenged the planter class's patriarchal society. The women called for a convention to "discuss the social, civil, and religious condition and rights of women" for the right to vote and to be treated equal to men. Elizabeth Cady Stanton published and read her *Declaration of Sentiments* to a crowd of three hundred men and women at the Seneca Falls Convention. Nearly one hundred in attendance signed her document, including William Lloyd Garrison, Lucretia Mott and a runaway slave turned orator and autobiographer, Frederick Douglass. Female agitators continued to hold conferences and demand their rights until the outbreak of war in 1861.

The planters of South Carolina's rice coast certainly loved their wives, mothers and daughters, but they believed that women occupied a different place in society than men in several ways. They held that women were to be honored for educating and raising children, providing a moralistic model for the family unit, running the homestead and serving and supporting their husbands' careers. The planters' notion of paternalism required them to shield the women in their lives from politics and economic concerns so as to keep them untarnished from the anxieties of business. As a result, gentlemen had their social clubs and societies where they could address business and politics, drink alcohol, use foul language and smoke cigars outside the home and away from their wives and daughters without offending their ears and noses. Although they attempted to shield their wives from business and politics, southern ladies, whether they liked it or not, lived right in the middle of their planter-husbands' agri-businesses. They were still burdened with traditional duties of wife of one and mother of many. Women helped supervise the slave labor force; nursed the sick, gave out rations of clothing and medicines; cut out garments; sewed; spun; and knitted.[36]

One Georgetown merchant from this period explained the demeanor and lack of political involvement among the ladies of Georgetown: "Politics were rather ignored in the drawing room, not because the ladies were supposed to be ignorant or out of sympathy with the questions of the day (on the contrary they rather cultivated a taste for public affairs), but as a matter of good form, because Southern Gallantry held that social occasions should be devoted mainly to the amusement of polite society."[37]

In an article in the *Winyah Observer*, "A Good Wife," the author wrote, "The Place of Women is eminently at the fireside. It is at home that you must see her to know what she is. It is less material what she is abroad; but what she is in the family circle is all important.[38] Other articles in the same journal, such as "Woman: Her Mission and Destiny" and "Diffusion of Christianity" and a poem in the same newspaper titled, "The Worth of a Woman," reinforced the female position in planter society.[39] On November 1, 1848, *Winyah Observer* published "Domestic Training," which advised women how to train their daughters to become good wives, and "Women," which explained their role in uplifting their husbands and helping to keep them focused on his trade by taking care of them[40]

The *Pee Dee Times*, the most prominent Georgetown newspaper of the 1850s, promoted the same mentality in a series of articles such as "A Wife's Devotion; or the Chivalry of Love," "A Receipt [Recipe] for Getting a Husband," "Devotion of a True Woman" and "Marrying Advice to Ladies."[41]

In an article titled, "How to Treat a Wife," the newspaper explained how a man should act toward his wife. Men must be patient—"you may have great trials and perplexities in your business with the world; but do not therefore carry to your home a clouded or contracted brow."[42]

The world the planters created inspired boys to become country gentlemen who mandated a society where girls supported the men in their lives rather than competed with them as equals. Their children started their formal education early and learned the art of manners, grace and conversation. Ladies married young, bore several children and expected their husbands to head the household.

Another assault on the patriarchal structure of the planters was the temperance movement, an undertaking to limit or ban the use of alcohol. The American Temperance Society started in 1826 with the intention of "saving the American family," and by the 1840s, it consisted of more than 8,000 local groups with more than 1.5 million members who had taken the pledge to abstain from consuming alcohol. Most rice planters enjoyed their brandy and cigars, wine, champagne and spirits. They consumed spirits at home and at their social clubs and society meetings, which were always occasions for celebration.

Eleazer Waterman, proprietor of the *Georgetown American* and later the *Winyah Observer*, explained that his paper would publish the views of all and not conform to support any agenda.[43] He published "The Drinking, Vending and Making Ardent Spirits," "The Temperance Oath" by Mary L. Gardner and, later, the Washingtonian's Temperance Oath.[44] Georgetown rice planter John Izard Middleton explained the planters' view of temperance, which, like most other issues, was based on their view of small, localized government: "I am opposed to a prohibitory law against the sale of ardent spirits. I deplore the evils which arise from the excessive indulgence in the use of strong drink, but fear those evils are beyond the reach of legislation."[45]

To the planter class, the abolitionist crusade was the largest, most visible, concentrated and dangerous reform movement spawned by the Second Great Awakening. The abolitionist movement originally began during the colonial period under the tutelage of the Quakers but spread throughout the North. Abolitionists' publications ran from the mundane, which simply asked for the release of slaves, to the radical. Boston free man of color David Walker was among the most radical. He called for a race war in his 1829 publication *Walker's Appeal* to free slaves. William Lloyd Garrison, the radical proprietor of the *Liberator* magazine, proposed that the virtuous New Englanders should secede from the United States if the federal government would not intervene and end slavery. Garrison's publications, as well as other abolitionist papers, were banned from the mail south of the Mason-Dixon line. At the same time, the United States House of Representatives adopted a "gag rule" on the issue of slavery from 1836 to 1844. The Senate was still open to debate the "peculiar institution," but the House, which was dominated by the northeastern states due to their population, banned discussing or debating the issue.

By the 1830s, the abolitionist movement became more centralized. William Lloyd Garrison and his abolitionist friends formed the American Antislavery Society, a national organization with branches throughout the North and West determined to end slavery in the United States. Some radical abolitionists refused to eat rice or sugar, wear cotton clothing or smoke tobacco because they were all produced by slave labor. By the 1840s, other abolitionists openly defied the fugitive slave laws by assisting runaways along the Underground Railroad, a system of safe houses along trails leading north. Abolitionists claimed that they were serving a higher power and law while they cognitively plotted and willfully broke the law by instilling and promoting insurrection, as well as by aiding runaways and their guides on their journey to northern states and Canada.

By the 1840s, major reforms of the Second Great Awakening were in full swing and picking up momentum in the Northeast and West. Wilderness utopian transcendentalist writers protested American ideals, social structure and organization as they championed civil disobedience to the law. They not only protested the values of the planter class but also retreated in protest from the demands of the new industrial world as well. Fredrika Bremer, a Swedish woman who stayed at Joel Roberts Poinsett's White House Plantation on the Pee Dee River when she visited the United States, boasted that she introduced him to transcendentalist literature. When she read Ralph Waldo Emerson to him, Poinsett explained how he felt that the transcendentalists were "unpractical" and criticized the entire literary movement. His antagonism prompted Bremer to say, "It is remarkable how very little, or not at all, the authors of the Northern States, even the best of them, are known in the South."[46]

Other reforms of the era stemmed from the personal experiences of the reformers. When Dorothea Dix visited a prison in Massachusetts, she was inspired to lead a movement for prison and asylum reforms. Still another movement, the push for anti-dueling legislation, drew particular distain from the planter class. In 1838, former South Carolina governor and Georgetown resident John Lyde Wilson published his chivalrous pamphlet on dueling, *The Code of Honor*. In Wilson's work, men of similar social status were encouraged to settle their differences in acts of combat. Still another Second Great Awakening reform proposed by northern citizens was a nationalized education system designed to assimilate immigrants. The local planters did not see a nationalized education system as a reform. They created their own education system through the Winyah Indigo Society, which educated sons and daughters of planters—merchants and yeoman farmers alike—in history, languages, the arts and science. Collectively, these reforms infuriated the conservative planters, who yearned for small localized government and a return to the social norms of their fathers' revolution.

The young men who matured to be the great planters of the antebellum era experienced these challenges firsthand. They grew up seeing their very civilization, social structure and values challenged by the ever-growing and ever-changing northern states. As a result, they developed a defensive posture to these deviations. The conservative southern mindset that surrounded their civilization was fostered by a stagnant population growth and the lack of immigration to the South. Spawned by the social modifications of the day taking place throughout the North, the planters and citizens of Georgetown and Horry looked inward and prepared for a life struggle to save their civilization, a struggle that would, like the English Civil War of the 1640s, once again pit Puritan against Cavalier.

Chapter 3

Southern Nationalism Taking Shape

A well-regulated militia, composed of the body of the people, trained in arms, is the best most natural defense of a free country.
–James Madison

While the nullification controversy unfolded, President Andrew Jackson made war on the Bank of the United States. In reaction to bank president Nicholas Biddle supporting the newly formed Whig Party (an alliance of Calhoun and Clay supporters to unseat Jackson and his supporters), Jackson convinced Congress to not renew the bank's charter.[47] The Second Bank of the United States was created as part of Henry Clay's American System. In a failed attempt to promote more competition and democracy in banking and break up what he saw as a growing monopoly on American wealth by the bank and its investors, Jackson withdrew all government funds from the bank. To promote greater competition in banking, he divided American funds and deposited them in various "pet banks." These banks quickly overextended credit to investors, and many of them collapsed. Therefore, the financial Panic of 1837 was a direct result of Jackson's war on the Bank of the United States, as well as over-speculation in western railroads, land and slaves.

Martin Van Buren was President Andrew Jackson's hand-picked successor who inherited a slumping economy from his mentor and was unable to resolve the financial dilemma. Van Buren's attempt to remedy the banking crisis was his Independent Treasury Plan. In the strategy, Van

Buren tied up United States money in regional banks. It seemed like a good idea to local planters, who championed states' rights, but it did not solve the economic problem completely. The *Georgetown American* hailed Martin Van Buren's Independent Treasury Plan as a "Second American Revolution" because it protected the people from the large bankers. The newspaper noted, "The Independent Treasury bill keeps people's money where it should be and kept from the wants of the government alone and not for the benefit of the speculators."[48]

In 1840, President Martin Van Buren, a Democrat, lost his bid for reelection to war hero William Henry Harrison, the first Whig president of the United States. At that time, the population of Georgetown was 18,264, of which 2,281 were free and 15,983 were enslaved.[49] Georgetown was a bustling little seaport whose influence, though not unified yet into one voice in political, social and economic affairs of South Carolina, was expanding.

The *Georgetown American* (another pro-Union newspaper) succeeded the *Georgetown Union* in November 9, 1839, with William Chapman as the editor. In the first edition, the newspaper explained that all topics except religion and abolitionism would be discussed. The *Georgetown American* printed lots of world news and history but not much politics or local news. Its motto was "Nothing extenuate…nor aught set down in malice." Eleazer Waterman had become the publisher by December 9, 1840, and eventually gained full ownership of the paper. Waterman was from Connecticut. He ran a variety of businesses in town and served in various positions in local government, including intendant (mayor) of the town. The paper ceased publication in March 1841, and Chapman died the following August. One week later, on March 10, 1841, Waterman rolled out the *Winyah Observer* with his son, Eleazer Waterman Jr. Later, J.W. Tarbox joined the production.

The *Winyah Observer* was not politically charged at the time, but it did encourage citizens to get involved in organizations, societies and clubs. In an article titled, "The Welfare of Our Town," the editor reminded the readers that they must "serve the community."[50]

Perhaps the greatest service that one could provide to his or her community was to serve in the local militia. The South Carolina legislature passed the Basic Patrol Law in December 1839 to protect the people from slave insurrections and domestic and foreign forces. Two years later, in 1841, Georgetown's two beat companies of the Lower Battalion, known as the upper and lower beats, consolidated.[51] All told, Georgetown had four units: the Georgetown Rifle Guards (incorporated on December 20, 1826), the Columbian Blues, the Washington Greys and the Wee Nee Dragoons.[52]

At this time, Major Richard Lathers commanded the Lower Battalion of the South Carolina Thirty-First Regiment, which consisted of four "beats": Black Mingo, Pee Dee, Georgetown and Santee. The militia drilled in "beats" but got together for a few full battalion drills per year at muster fields such as those at Watchesaw Plantation (now known as Wachesaw) and the Socastee Bridge. The citizen-soldiers also manned the voting precincts on Election Day and met for patriotic displays such as the celebration of Independence Day on July 4 and for George Washington's birthday.[53] Richard Lathers stated that he was not quite of age when he was elected major of the Thirty-First Regiment but recalled that "[c]ompany, battalion and regimental trainings were frequent, and, in addition, every two years all the officers from Sergeants to Generals were assembled for ten days in camp to be drilled in the requirements of soldier under the direction of the Governor of the State."[54]

In February 1841, Georgetown celebrated the anniversary of George Washington's birth. A procession gathered at the Market House and, at 9:00 a.m., began a march to Prince George Winyah Church. The Wee Nee Dragoons (commanded by Major Richard Lathers) led the procession, followed by the Georgetown Rifle Guards (Infantry), closely trailed by Robert F.W. Allston (orator of the day), followed by United States officers, the town council, the Committee of Arrangements, members of the Winyah Indigo Society, members of the Winyah Masonic Lodge and the citizenry. Allston addressed the crowd when the procession reached the church.[55] This display of patriotism was very common in Georgetown during the era. Flags and fireworks prominently filled the air, and citizens proudly wore their red, white and blue clothing and accoutrements.

A few months later, on July 4, Lathers served as the orator of the day for the town council of Georgetown's Independence Day celebration. He recalled that there was a military and civic parade that marched from the old town hall through the principal streets of Georgetown to the Methodist church. There the band played the "soul-stirring hymn Hail Columbia." Lathers gave his speech, and the preacher offered a passionate prayer and a patriotic oration.[56]

The *Winyah Observer* printed nearly one hundred articles from 1840 through 1850 on the Wee Nee Dragoons and the various infantry militia units. Some articles were simply advertisements for members to meet at certain locations for review and drill, and others were reports of patriotic militaristic displays such as "Military Parade at Black Mingo" and "Celebration of the 22nd."[57]

The age of Whig presidents William Henry Harrison and John Tyler was relatively calm and without great sectional conflict, but the recollection of the power-hungry Federalist Party was still close in memory. One politically charged article from this period pertained to the proceedings from the Democratic States' Rights Party in June 1841. The article complained that the old Alexander Hamilton "Federalist ideals of big government were surfacing again and must be fought."[58]

The pressing matter of the early and mid-1840s was the issue of Texas annexation. Southerners began to call for the annexation of Texas in 1836 shortly after the upstart republic gained independence from Mexico. The issue of admitting Texas into the Union renewed the sectional contest and quickly became the primary battleground between North and South.

In May 1844, Baltimore held the Democratic National Convention to determine which of the three candidates would be the party's standard bearer. The Georgetown delegation of Richard Lathers, Eleazer Waterman, Colonel McKay, William J. Howard and General James M. Commander (all members of the militia except Waterman) were the only South Carolinians to attend the meeting. The group arrived in Baltimore two days before the convention started and began to lay the groundwork for southern cooperation concerning secession. Since Georgetown ended up having the only delegates at the meeting, the group was given the authority to cast all of South Carolina's nine votes. It was common to hear the General Commander say, "South Carolina casts nine votes" for this measure or this candidate. John Van Buren said that when his father was defeated for the nomination, "It is humiliating indeed to be flogged by that South Carolina cat-of-nine-tails from Georgetown, South Carolina, wielding the suffrage of his whole State."[59] Van Buren did not support the annexation of Texas. The *Winyah Observer* reported, "Martin Van Buren has produced much disappointment with many of his Southern and Western friends but three days ago, [we] are now disposed to drop him and look for another candidate."[60]

Texas was instrumental to the preservation of the entire economy of the United States, and its annexation was not simply steeped in regional bias. Most importantly to Texas, the Independent Republic was fearful of being reconquered by Mexico and had not only offered the United States the opportunity to annex it but also extended the same offer to England since the United States was slow to act. Had England annexed Texas, England would no longer need southern cotton, and the entire economy of the United States would have been placed in jeopardy. Raw cotton represented more than 50 percent of all American exports by the 1840s.

Rice Produced in the United States in 1840

Region	*Rice Produced in 1840*
Georgetown District	36,360,000 pounds
Charleston District	11,938,750 pounds
Beaufort District	5,629,402 pounds
Colleton District	5,483,533 pounds
South Carolina Total	**59,411,685 pounds**
United States Total	**80,841,422 pounds**

In a show of solidarity among the Lowcountry planters and newspapers, the *Winyah Observer* agreed with the *Charleston Mercury*. The *Winyah Observer* cried out, "[T]here cannot be any reasonable objection to the annexation on the part of any of the states. To the South the annexation is of vital importance, in connection with her institutions, especially as the North is constantly aiming at dissolution of the Union through the slave question, and excessive protective duties."[61]

Fearful that the South would outvote the manufacturing states and end all tariffs, leaving the manufacturing sector vulnerable to competition from imports, the New England states once again called for secession. The *Winyah Observer* saw the opportunity to chime in on the northern fear of lost tariff protection and calmly appealed for cooler heads to prevail: "As to the tariff, the whole country is in favor of a reasonable one, and almost any that is not prohibitory, can be reconciled to all parties in a week's debate on the subject with honest politicians."[62]

On the Fourth of July, the Pee Dee community celebrated American independence in grand style at the Pee Dee muster field. After the audience was seated, John Harleston Read Jr. (Pee Dee planter and representative) commenced the annual exercises by reading the Declaration of Independence and giving a few pertinent "remarks and reflections upon the causes which led to the publication of that manifesto and declaration which has been so justly styled the character of Liberty." After the reading and patriotic speech "the company partook of a very bountiful repast [picnic]." Apparently, a rumor began to circulate that Pee Dee senator Robert F.W. Allston was soon to arrive and would address the crowd. Allston did eventually arrive and did indeed give an address. He spoke of the need to annex Texas, and by the time he was through with his oration, the crowd had given up nine rounds of cheers. The newspaper reported that there "was not a single instance of intoxication, and not a quarrel, while we remained on the grounds."[63]

Later in the month, the South Carolina Lowcountry again launched a secession movement from the federal government in reaction to yet another tariff increase (1842) and because John C. Calhoun failed to win the Whig Party nomination. Henry Clay won the nomination and promised to block the annexation of Texas in fear of war with Mexico. At the Bluffton, South Carolina Convention, under the "secession oak," South Carolinians further complained that Presidents Andrew Jackson, Martin Van Buren, William Henry Harrison and John Tyler all had the opportunities to annex Texas to the Union but refused to admit the republic for no other reason than the fact that it wanted to enter the country as a slave state. The *Charleston Mercury* helped stoke the fire of discontent in Georgetown and throughout the Lowcountry by warning of the double threat of tariffs and abolitionism. If Texas was not going to be annexed, Lowcountry South Carolinians touted that they should secede from the Union and start their own country.[64]

With the election of the Democratic candidate James K. Polk in 1844, outgoing Whig president John Tyler, who was snubbed by his party and not nominated for reelection, finally convinced Congress to admit Texas into the Union as a mandate of the people. With the annexation of Texas complete, the balance of power in the Senate temporarily leaned in favor of the South (fifteen slave states to thirteen free). There was a lot of talk at this time of annexing parts of, if not all of, Canada to keep the northern frontiersmen, as well as the northern politicians and industrialists, happy.[65] None of Canada was brought into the United States, but President Polk made a deal to split the Oregon Country with England, giving the United States another injection of expansionist nationalism.

As soldiers rushed to enlist for the coming war with Mexico, Horry District formed its own cavalry unit. In the first regimental election for the Eighth South Carolina Cavalry since the Horry District created the Horry Hussars, Lieutenant Eliphalet H. Miller defeated incumbent Major B.A. Coachman to become major of the lower squadron. The lower squadron consisted of Georgetown's Wee Nee Dragoons, the Black Mingo Light Dragoons, the Kingstree Light Dragoons and the Horry Hussars.[66]

By 1845, regional political discontent had spilled over the border of Georgetown and was plainly visible in Horry District. On Independence Day 1845, *Winyah Observer* reporter and editor Eleazer Waterman traveled to Conwayboro, where the people held a great demonstration in honor of American independence. The day started with the formation of a military and civilian procession in the following order: Horry Hussars, beat company, chaplain, orator and reader and, finally, local citizens. Colonel James Beaty of the Horry Hussars led the procession to the Methodist church on the corner of Main Street and Fifth Avenue. B.M. Singleton read the Declaration of Independence under an American flag, which waved seventy-six feet over the gathering. The entire crowd burst into applause several times during the reading of Thomas Jefferson's famous treatise. After the reading, the cavalry and many of the inhabitants of the town retired to a shady grove of towering oaks near the Methodist church. There the group dined on a meal prepared by Timothy Cooper while they were entertained by the drilling display of Colonel James Beaty and the Horry Hussars.[67]

After the drill and meal, Benjamin A. Thomson, assisted by Colonel James Beaty and Dr. William Kelland Cuckon, presided over further ceremonies. During the afternoon, the people listened to several toasts. Thirteen regular toasts (one for each of the original thirteen colonies) were offered before the floor was open to volunteer tributes. Among the planned thirteen toasts, some were patriotic memorials to recently deceased president Andrew Jackson, the memories of the American Revolutionary soldiers and leaders, the seated governor and seated president of the United States, the strength of women and foreigners such as the Marquis de Lafayette, Johann von Robais, Baron de Kalb and Casimir Pulaski who helped the Americans win their independence. The remaining planned speeches were fiery and poignant toasts levied against the federal government. Shouting out against the northern-dominated House of Representatives, which was by this time operating under a gag rule that forbade the discussion of the institution of slavery, one speaker said, "The House of Representatives of the United States, a diseased body that requires more purging and less pay." Shortly thereafter, a speaker celebrated the Senate of the United States by stating, "The Senate of the United States, a wholesome check upon the noisy demagogues that infest the hall of the House of Representatives."[68]

Next, the floor was open to voluntary speeches. Among those was one offered by Dr. Cuckon, who took the opportunity to attack the free school system in South Carolina; he stated, "The free school system of the State, totally defective, may it be speedily revised and reformed; it requires prompt legislative action to give it that efficiency it now wants." A short time later, Colonel N.G. Rich offered a toast to the Horry Hussars: "The citizen soldiery of Horry, brave generous and hospitable, with such men for defenders we have nothing to fear from foreign aggression." George Fisk volunteered the next toast. He attacked England's abolitionists when he said,

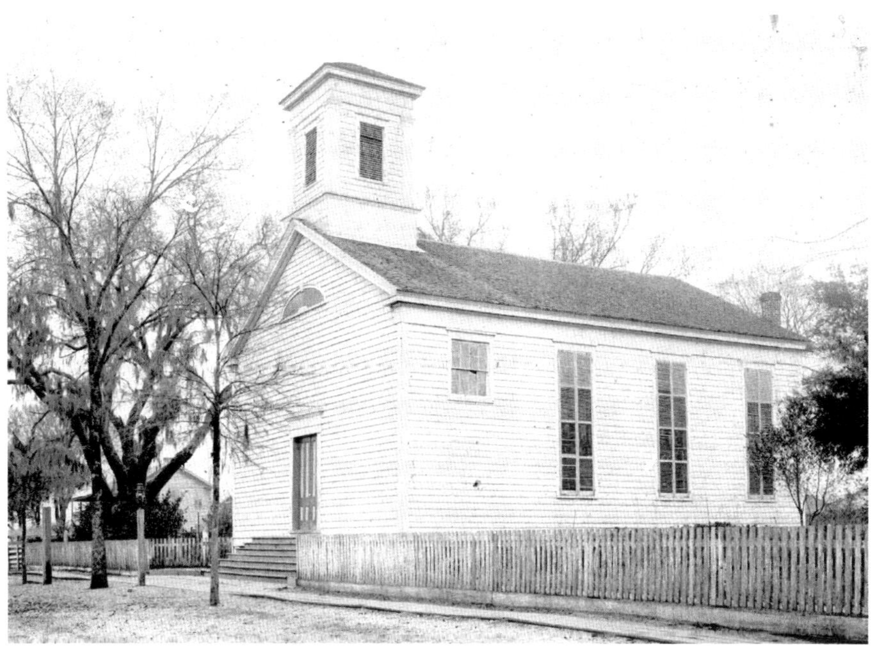

Conway Methodist Church. *Courtesy of the Horry County Historical Society.*

"British Abolitionists—let them feed and clothe their white slaves half as well as we do our black ones." A few more citizens offered toasts, and then George Fisk rose again to offer a militaristically inspired toast. He said, "The Conwayborough Invincibles, equally true to the cartridge box, or the ballot box." Eleazer Waterman of the *Winyah Observer* wrote, "The day passed off harmoniously." After a few more toasts were offered, the community drank toasts moistened by "a grateful and cooling beverage, flavored by the golden fruit of the Tagus."[69]

While Horry had a politically charged Fourth of July celebration, Georgetown passed the holiday in much milder fashion. Richard Lathers read the Declaration of Independence to the crowd, and Colonel Peter Waties Fraser gave a patriotic oration to the Wee Nee Dragoons and Georgetown citizens at the Methodist church. The *Winyah Observer* did not record any of the toasts or oratories offered at the occasion, but it did remark that "republics are ungrateful and pay little regard to the sages of the ages."[70]

Meanwhile, in the Northwest, settlers flocked to Iowa and Wisconsin. The two territories would not become states until 1846 and 1848, respectively, to restore the balance of power in the Senate. For a short time, the South had the edge in the Senate, but there was a lull in the sectional struggle. The *Winyah Observer* filled its pages with articles on revolutions in South and Central America, war in Europe and Asia Minor, the opium trade in China, worldwide catastrophes such as earthquakes, how to improve morals at home, poetry, reminiscences of the past, patriotism, political speeches, advertisements, the politics of Florida and Texas, news from England and the very real prospect of war with Mexico. Mexico had claimed that it would reconquer Texas and warned the United States that annexation would mean war.

One month before the outbreak of the Mexican-American War, the *Winyah Observer* alerted its readers to two major issues. The first was the proud announcement that England had repealed its Corn Laws. England's tariffs on all grains were introduced as a protection measure against Henry Clay's American System, which imposed the first tariff in United States history. With the repeal of the Corn Laws, southerners hoped that the United States would follow suit by reducing tariffs on manufactured goods. The other alarming issue concerned Texas's expanding cotton production. With a steady increase in production, Texans were buying up slaves from other American states, causing a scarcity of labor and driving up the price of production and thus reducing profits.[71]

In April 1846, the United States entered into war with Mexico over the annexation of Texas, and again the nation came to a crossroads. A few short months after the onset of war, Pennsylvania's Democrat senator David Wilmot shattered the short period of nationalism when he proposed the Wilmot Proviso. In his proviso, Wilmot suggested that all land gained in the war be closed to slavery since the land was currently slave-free under Mexico's control. Wilmot claimed that allowing slavery to enter the region was not promoting democracy to the region, but rather promoting the "slavocracy" of the South. Southerners assumed that western expansion would naturally continue the extension of the Missouri Compromise dividing line between the North and the South to the West Coast. The measure easily passed the House of Representatives, as representation in the House is based on population, but did not pass the Senate, where each state had two votes. Although the measure did not pass, it caused a reopening of political and mental wounds between North and South and showed that the United States, although a nation at war with Mexico, was anything but united.

In February 1847, the Wilmot Proviso was again introduced to the legislature. The measure once again passed the House of Representatives but was again defeated in the Senate. In an article titled, "Ruin of the

Slaveholder and the Slave," the *Winyah Observer* reminded its readers of the ramifications of the Wilmot Proviso if the South did not expand with the rest of the Union. In April, the paper printed a much more precise and scathing attack on the Wilmot Proviso when it stated, "The Wilmot Proviso is an attack upon the constitutional rights of all the states, and the Democracy of this state." By this time, the newspaper had replaced the slogan "Published every Wednesday at Three dollars per Annum" with "We will cling to the Temple of our Liberties, and if it must fall, we will perish amidst the ruins."[72] The times were truly changing; the region was radicalizing.

Throughout the war effort, the newspaper often attempted to discount Wilmot's Proviso and remain patriotic. The paper published several articles on the Battles of Vera Cruz, Buena Vista and Cerro Gordo, as well as guerrilla warfare on the Rio Grande.[73] Although the bonds of union were strained between the regions of the country in general, one Georgetown citizen recalled the patriotism of local veterans during the Mexican-American War who fought together and made their state proud: "It is to this South Carolina heritage of a Marion, a Moultrie, a Henry, a Pickens, and a Sumter that is due in a large measure the state pride which sent into the fields of Mexico the fearless Palmetto Regiment led by Colonel Butler, who fell in the battle at the head of his troops."[74] Although the locals cheered for their boys who fought against Mexico, the problems that separated the regions were lying just below the surface of patriotism, as the issues of tariffs and regional differences were growing ever more divisive.

Tired of enduring the continued assault on slavery in a defensive manner, the *Winyah Observer* went on the offensive and published a scornful article titled, "A Day at Lowell" to expose factory working conditions in the North and to reinforce its validation of slavery. The article thoroughly explained how twenty-five thousand workers (nine thousand of whom were mill girls between the ages of nine and fourteen) lived in the upstart textile mill town of Lowell, Massachusetts. It explained how the mill town had twenty-four churches, which took roll at service, and noted that church attendance was mandatory for employment. The accusations continued. Workers lived in cramped barracks designed exclusively for the employees by the employers, who also provided stores to sell the employees everything they needed. At the end of the week, men could expect $4.00, and women earned a miniscule $1.75 for their six-day, twelve- to fourteen-hour commitment to Lowell. The paper asked its readers how the factory system was anything but an industrial model for slavery, as employees gave all of their money back to the factory through purchases and rent.[75]

On February 2, 1848, the Mexican-American War officially ended with the Treaty of Guadalupe Hidalgo. In a last-ditch effort to pass the Wilmot Proviso, northern politicians again attempted to pass the measure as part of the treaty. Again the Wilmot Proviso failed; however, fear of federal government legislation such as the Wilmot Proviso caused the Eighth South Carolina Cavalry and the various South Carolina Infantry regiments to hold regular military exercises throughout the Pee Dee region that spring. Reminiscent of the Boston countryside in the spring of 1775, the Pee Dee region was alive with military preparations in the spring of 1845. The Kingstree Light Dragoons and the Thirty-First Infantry Regiment (Upper Battalion) drilled in Kingstree on May 5, and the Wee Nee Dragoons and the Thirty-First Infantry Regiment (Lower Battalion) trained in Georgetown on May 9. The Horry Hussars drilled with the Thirty-Second Infantry Regiment in Conwayborough on May 13, and the Marion Light Dragoons trained with the Third Infantry Regiment at the Marion Courthouse on May 16. All militias lined up for review at noon, and drill followed.[76]

As the election of 1848 drew closer, the people of Georgetown and Horry again looked forward to positive change. Fear arose when word arrived that England (the South's largest consumer of cotton) was attempting to avoid the United States market by growing the fiber in its own empire—most recently in the northwestern part of Australia.[77] Although Georgetown and the Lowcountry were economically tied to rice, the South in general was knotted to cotton; with the loss of the British market, the general economy of the South would collapse.

That spring, the Democratic Party started holding meetings in Georgetown, and by late May, the Whig Party had followed suit.[78] In August, the *Winyah Observer* published an editorial titled, "North and South: Van Buren, Cass and Taylor: Which Can the South Support?" Colonel John Harleston Read Jr. stated that he supported Zachary Taylor because Taylor "has 300 slaves which he intends to keep." He also reminded the citizens that if the South does not band together to all vote for Taylor, the election could go to the House of Representatives, which the North dominated in numeric superiority. Read concluded that Northerners with their "fanaticism would elect Van Buren" to further their agenda of Free Soil.[79] Fortunately for Read and his supporters, Taylor did win the election.

Despite Taylor's victory in the election, the mistrust created by the Wilmot Proviso compelled the South Carolina legislature to unanimously resolve that the time for discussion with the federal government had passed and that it was time to seek a union with the other southern states. The elder statesman John C. Calhoun made it very clear when he said, "Though the Union is dear to us, our honor and our liberty are dearer."[80]

It seemed as though South Carolina had finally had enough debate on secession and was ready to act. In spite of the strong rhetoric by the state legislature, the *Winyah Observer* toned down its slogan in February 1849 to "Devoted to news, General Intelligence, Miscellany &c, &c." This was also the first issue under the new ownership of Waterman and Tarbox, with Benjamin Henry Wilson as editor.[81] As implied in the slogan, the paper focused more on agriculture and history and less on politics for a short time. Articles on Chinese etiquette, parental examples, ladies' concerns, France, the Roman Empire and gold fever in the West filled its pages.[82]

In just one four-year administration, President James K. Polk nearly doubled the size of the United States. Polk annexed Texas; fought and won the Mexican-American War, which brought in the entire Southwest with the Treaty of Guadalupe Hidalgo; and made a deal with England to divide the disputed Oregon Territory. With Manifest Destiny complete (the belief that the United States should own all the land from the Atlantic to the Pacific), land-hungry Americans now looked north and south in the hopes of expanding their dominion over the entire Western Hemisphere.

In 1849, General Winfield Scott (one of the great heroes of the Mexican-American War) renewed the call for a land grab for more northern territory. In an article titled, "On Annexation of Canada," General Scott called for further expansion in order to spur on nationalism and settle sectional problems. It was a safe time to call for annexation of Canada since it was breaking away from England. Scott claimed that expansion would serve all those involved, as the United States would be expanding its prosperity to Canadians. There were thirty states in the Union at that time—fifteen free and fifteen slave states. The balance of power in the Senate was gridlocked between the divergent regions.[83]

While Scott was calling for wider nationalism, the Georgetown and Horry Districts called for Southern Nationalism. On April 9, 1849, leading statesmen of the Georgetown District met in the city of Georgetown to discuss John C. Calhoun's call for a meeting of southern states in Jackson, Mississippi, to plan a resistance to the federal government. The group called for unified stern opposition to the government when it noted that "the Government of the Confederacy cannot of right impose upon the people of any States or territory any particular scheme of internal policy, except to the extent of the authority expressly delegated to that government by the Constitution of the United States." The assembly expressed its love for the "Union entered into by our fathers we are ardently attached; for it was a Union of friendly communities for common purpose of mutual defense." But, the committee continued, "when we witness the war ill-disguised which is waging against us under the screen of this Union, we cannot but regard it with alienation and distrust." The group reminded the people of Georgetown that each of the great sections of the country had its own "peculiar scheme" of civilization and vowed to never attempt to influence decisions made in the North asserting that each section of the country must be "permitted to work out for itself the great problem of its political salvation undisturbed by the other."[84]

The committee then adopted six resolutions designed to bind the southern states together in defiance to the federal government. They called for a confederacy of "co-States" for mutual "maintenance of our rights." The most pressing of the resolutions stated, "That the adoption by the Federal Government of the measure in reference to the Territories called the Wilmot Proviso, would absolve us from our federal obligations, and compel us and our co-States to resort to such means of defense, as the great law of self-preservation may require." As a final measure, Chairman Robert F.W. Allston appointed a group of thirteen (which included Joshua John Ward, Dr. Edward Thomas Heriot, Dr. John D. Magill and Benjamin Henry Wilson) to constitute a Committee of Correspondence and a Committee of Safety for Georgetown.[85]

At the same time, the people of Conwayborough called for Southern Nationalism at a large meeting held in support of the southern delegates in Congress who opposed the Wilmot Proviso. Peter Vaught Sr. served as chair of the meeting, and Colonel James Beaty and Benjamin E. Sessions served as secretaries. Vaught appointed Henry Buck, Thomas Randall, Thomas Sessions and five others to a committee to draft resolutions expressive of the sentiments of the southern delegates in Congress. John McQueen addressed the assembly "in a very forcible and impressive speech" and condemned the "encroachments upon the institutions of the South by the Abolitionists, now called the Free Soil Party." With great passion, McQueen promoted Southern Nationalism when he declared that "if the South should submit to the degradation and insult involved in the passage of the Wilmot Proviso, they would be recreant to their past history, their past glory, and the memory of their fathers." The great fear was that if the Wilmot Proviso became law, the people of the South would not be able to expand with the rest of the Union and would thereafter soon be outvoted in every regional vote in the Senate.

The assembly passed a few resolutions. One was an open call to arms. "Resolved, that we will cordially unite with our fellow-citizens of the Southern States in any measure of resistance that may be deemed advisable to check this war of aggression and officious intermeddling with our peculiar institutions."

After the reading and submission of the preamble and resolutions submitted by the committee, all proposals were adopted. Next, a Committee of Safety was established. Some members of the Committee of Safety included Honorable Joel B. Skipper, Henry Buck, Thomas Randall, Daniel W. Oliver, Pugh Floyd, Ulric A. Delettere, Benjamin E. Sessions, Thomas Beaty and John Tillman.[86]

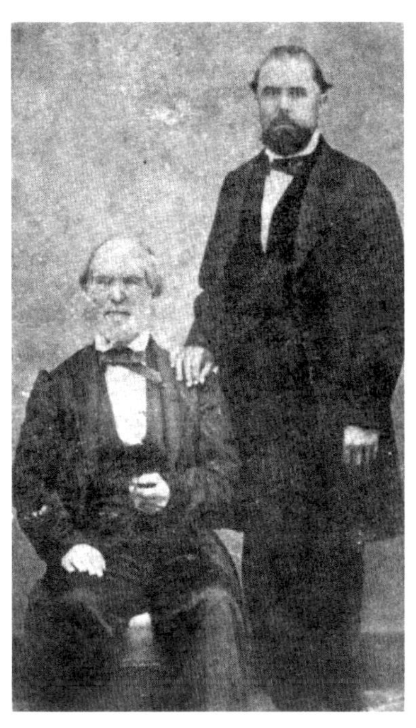

Peter Vaught Sr. and Peter Vaught Jr.
Courtesy of the Horry County Historical Society.

That summer, the *Winyah Observer* reported on the Independence Day celebration in Johnsonville. After the reading of the Declaration of Independence, fiery oratory and regular toasts, B.J. Bradley toasted the Rough and Ready Dragoons: "If called to the service of their country we are sure that their courage and conduct will equal their generosity and hospitality." P.B. Mouzon toasted the Dragoons as well: "The Rough and Ready Dragoons—The bone and sinew of Muddy Creek—they are the ornament of our district in peace, and in war will prove themselves the right arm of its defense."[87]

In Georgetown, the people celebrated the Fourth of July in grand patriotic fashion and once again focused on service to the community. The following societies and companies were invited to attend and form a procession in the following order: Wee Nee Dragoons, Georgetown Rifle Guards (with musical accompaniment), Hayne Lodge (League of Odd Fellows), Winyah Lodge of Free Masons, Winyah Indigo Society, Salamander Hook and Ladder Company and Winyah Axe Company. The citizens of Georgetown followed the organizations in the following order: the honorable intendent and the town council, reverends, clergy and finally the orator and reader. The procession began from the town hall at 11:00 a.m., continued up Front Street to Broad Street, followed Broad to Highmarket Street, traveled Highmarket to Screven Street and then followed Screven back to the courthouse. William W. Shackelford served as the marshal of the day.[88] Although the crowds waved the banner of patriotism on this auspicious day, the specter of secession was always lurking, the threat of disunion only a heartbeat away.

On July 25th, the *Winyah Observer* published an article titled, "Who Has Betrayed the South?" The essay accused former president John Quincy Adams as being the man to be blamed for the heated regional rivalry since he had passed high tariffs and as being anti-southern because the South did not support him or his father (John Adams) as presidents. The article also claimed that the northern Whigs were to blame because they were adopting the abolitionist stance—before that time, the abolitionists were just considered to be a bunch of regional extremists.[89]

On October 1, 1849, representatives from the southern states met in Jackson, Mississippi, to demand the end to slavery agitation in the northern states, curtail the Underground Railroad and encourage southerners to migrate west. At the end of the day, they agreed to reconvene in Nashville, Tennessee, in the summer of 1850 to form a Southern Confederacy if the agitation did not cease.[90] Also in 1849, Robert F.W. Allston represented South Carolina and served as a vice-president at the great Railroad Convention in Memphis, Tennessee.[91]

The 1850 census revealed that the population of the United States was continuing to expand at a disproportional rate. The United States at mid-century contained 23 million people, of which 7.25 million lived in the South. Within ten years, with the continued influx of German and Irish immigrants to the West and North, respectively, the population of the United States would grow to 31 million, of which roughly 9 million lived in the southern states (4 million as slaves).

At the dawn of the decade, southerners were completely enraged by the changes taking place in the North and with the way that northerners were attempting to enforce their ideas of reform on the country. The *Winyah Observer* published the article "The Slavery Question," which was a complete defense of the institution of slavery and the southern way of life.[92] With the South continuously closing in on itself in defense of its civilization, and having called for the Nashville Convention with all fifteen slaveholding states for the coming summer, northern reformers incessantly calling for change and the population in the western territories expanding and pushing for statehood, it appeared that the United States was careening toward insolvency, if not violence.

On January 29, 1850, in an attempt to diffuse the conflict between the regions, derail the Nashville Convention scheduled for June, avoid southern secession and possible civil war, Henry Clay introduced yet another compromise. Clay's Compromise of 1850, also known as the Omnibus Bill, included a strict fugitive slave law (which employed federal marshals to track down runaways and punish those involved in aiding and encouraging them); a ban on slave trading in Washington, D.C.; the admission of California as a free state; and popular sovereignty (the people choose if their state will become a free or slave state) in the land gained in the Mexican-American War.[93] Extremists on both sides criticized the effort.

South Carolina senator John C. Calhoun, very close to death and unable to deliver his own speech but still present in the Senate, proposed the Concurrent Majority. Modeled after the division of the Roman Empire's power base between Constantinople and Rome, Calhoun's plan proposed that the United States remain intact, but that the executive branch be shared by two presidents—one to look over the interests of the industrial North and one over the agricultural South.[94]

Two weeks after Clay offered his compromise, Georgetown's *True Republican* newspaper printed an article, "Southern Convention," about the prospect of secession at the upcoming Nashville Convention. Promoting southern nation building, the newspaper claimed that the South was out of options and urged the convention to vote for secession. The paper screamed out, "This is the only method left by which we can ward off the dishonor and degradation to which the North designs subjecting us. Let us therefore set the ball in motion, whose rolling is to accumulate the united strength of Southern patriotism and Southern intellect into a harmonious unity of action." The article explained that Southerners must unite to "drive the invader from the soil we hold dear—our native land."[95]

The countryside was filled with paramilitary actions in the spring of 1850. John Harleston Read Jr., lieutenant colonel of Lower Battalion of Thirty-First Regiment, South Carolina Militia, ordered the Georgetown Militia Company to meet at the market on the first day of March to elect new officers. The dragoons and infantry drilled and paraded after elections. In another article published the same day, by orders of Brigadier General J.M. Commander, the Thirty-Third Regiment paraded at Conwayborough on Saturday, March 3, 1850, and the Thirty-First Regiment paraded for review at Black Mingo on Tuesday, March 5. The Thirty-Second Regiment paraded on Tuesday, March 12, at the Marion Courthouse.[96]

Senator John C. Calhoun died on March 31, 1850, and Robert F.W. Allston eulogized the great statesman.[97] He began his oration by saying, "We all prized him for his matchless services in the public councils, his rare sagacity in discovering truth, and the transcendent power with which he elucidated it: his undying attachment to his native state, and his untiring efforts to vindicate her rights, and promote her welfare."[98] Allston reminded his audience that Calhoun had spent the better part of his public life fighting for a "Union of the South for the sake of the Union." He retold the people of Calhoun's many selfless posts in the government from the House of Representatives and Senate to the secretary of war, secretary of state and vice president under two presidents. He talked about Calhoun's struggles to fight against the tariffs and the Nullification Crisis, for which he was so admired in South Carolina. He said, "He died in the midst of a contest for Equality or Independence, nobly contending to the last for the rights of his native state, in common with the Southern States, against the grasping cupidity and unjust aggressions of a Northern majority."[99]

Allston extended his point by saying, "We contend for non-intervention; that the General government has no power to legislate thus partially, invidiously, oppressively; and insist upon the right of property; individual right to emigrate with our social institutions, and upon our rights as States, under the Constitution of the Union." He reminded the listeners that although Calhoun sometimes talked of secession, his efforts were always directed to the preservation of the Union, not its dissolution, and that secession was seen as a last resort to maintain the Constitutional rights of South Carolina and the South. In Calhoun's memory, Allston formally dedicated the people of Georgetown to his ideals and his causes when he said we "will maintain for the Southern States, their Equality, or Independence."[100]

Allston ended his eulogy by giving advice to the women of Georgetown and asked them to teach their children about him. As if preparing Calhoun for martyrdom, he cried out, "Daughters of Carolina weep not for him now, but tell your children to his illustrious example. Rest not till you have imparted to him a love of truth, justice, and benevolence; rest not till you have taught him to practice self-denial, self-control, and all the sublime precepts of the Gospel."[101]

Allston was not the only one to eulogize Calhoun; in fact, many of his political friends and adversaries lauded the great statesman. Calhoun's greatest adversary in the Senate was Daniel Webster. Webster eulogized him by saying, "He had the basis, the indispensable basis of all high character; and that was unspotted integrity and unimpeached honor. Firm in his purpose, perfectly patriotic and honest, I do not believe he had a selfish motive or a selfish feeling." He continued, "However he may have differed from others of us in his political opinions, or his political principles, those principles and those opinions will now descend to posterity under the sanction of a great name."[102]

In June 3–11, southern delegates met as planned at the Nashville Convention in Tennessee, but things had changed since the call for the meeting a year earlier. Only nine of the fifteen southern states invited to Nashville sent delegations (Virginia, Georgia, Tennessee, Alabama, Mississippi, Arkansas, Texas and Florida, as well as South Carolina) to the meeting, and the delegates sent were mostly interested in cooperation with the Union, not secession. Robert F.W. Allston of Georgetown and W.J. Hanna of Chesterfield served as delegates from the Fourth Congressional District, South Carolina.[103]

By the time the delegates finally met, the movement for secession had lost much of its momentum, but the gentlemen built relationships at the meeting that would later come to fruition. Robert F.W. Allston penned a letter to his son, Benjamin, then a cadet at West Point Military Academy, from the Nashville Convention. He wrote that he had made several new political allies in Nashville, where they met "respecting the course of legislation in congress on the subject of the territories acquired from Mexico by the close of the late war."[104] He wrote a letter to his wife from the same location in which he stated, "Unless the Northern people now come to be reasonable people, Revolution will be unavoidable. It were better to settle the matter now than to leave it to our children."[105]

Upon returning home from the Nashville Convention, South Carolina Lowcountry planters again beat the drum of secession and attempted to lead the state down the fiery path to disunion. As they had done in 1832 and 1844, many Lowcountry planters called on South Carolina to act alone. However, the two regions of the state continued to be at odds and remained divided among old lines: Lowcountry planters called for secession and upcountry farmers called for moderation and compromise. A divided South Carolina once again backed down from independence.

By the summer of 1850, the Horry District was quickly becoming noted for its strong political stance against the federal government of the United States. The *Charleston Courier*—perhaps convinced that the Horry District had become a hotbed for secession after the strong rhetoric at Independence Day celebrations in 1845, the anti–Wilmot Proviso meeting and the formation of the Committee of Safety—sent a reporter to Conwayborough on the Fourth of July 1850. As was customary for Conwayborough, an assembly formed downtown at the courthouse that walked in procession to the Methodist church. At the church, more than six hundred people assembled for the annual celebration of independence from Great Britain. Julius Anderson read the Declaration of Independence, and Colonel Thomas F. Gillespie gave an oration that reflected on the struggles of the Revolutionary era to the troubles of the day. After the proceedings at the Methodist church, the entire group removed to Colonel James Beaty's house, where they dined.

While they ate, Senator Joel B. Skipper read thirteen regular toasts. The regular toasts included "The Union: May it be as enduring as the fame of Washington is the sentiment of every true American heart" and "The Nashville Convention: Composed of patriotic men—ever ready to contribute to the glory and to uphold the rights of the South." Next, Skipper opened the floor to voluntary toasts. Colonel James Beaty responded with an ode to Southern Nationalism when he said, "The Palmetto State: True in war, true in peace, and ever watchful of the interests of the South." Major John Readmon followed Beaty by stating, "The Union without the Constitution is worse than Tyranny." Immediately following Readmon, attorney Thomas F. Gillespie rose to his feet and echoed John C. Calhoun's speech at the Jefferson Day banquet in 1832 when he said, "The Union: We prize it, but prize more the liberties it was intended to perpetuate." Several other gentlemen in attendance gave spirited speeches, such as James T. Duboise, who said, "May the spirit which animated the hearts of our fathers in '76 sustain their sons in '50, and the same glorious result will follow." The people of Horry celebrated for hours after the conclusion of the toasts. At dark, a torchlight parade proceeded back to the Methodist church for more oratory. "A brilliant display of fireworks concluded the exercises of the 4th of July at Conwayboro[ugh]."[106]

Clay's 1850 compromise passed the House of Representatives and Senate that summer and was signed by President Millard Fillmore in September 1850. California was immediately admitted to the Union and offset the balance of power. It appeared as though the impasse of 1850 was over and that the Union of unhappy states would remain united, at least on paper.

In the midst of the 1850 crisis, the *Winyah Observer* published articles such as "Slavery and the Constitution," in which the paper explained to its readers that slavery was legal in the Constitution and that the people of the South had the right to maintain the institution. The paper furthered the defense of slavery by stating that northern agitation of slavery would not cease and expressed the need for citizens to prepare to defend their civilization.[107] The

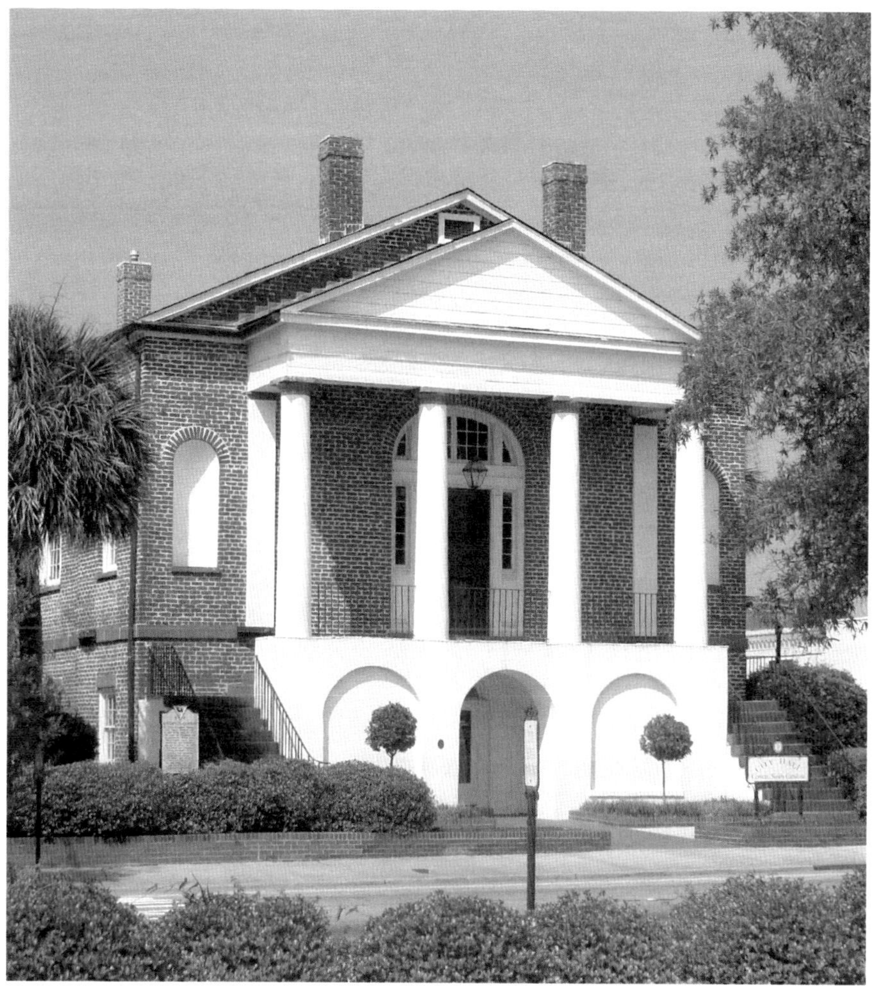

Conway Courthouse. *Courtesy of Horry County Historical Society.*

paper also published an article explaining that the design of the originators of the Nashville Convention was pure and patriotic, as they were meeting for secession in the name of defending the rights of all citizens as they were explained in the United States Constitution. Other articles focused on the lives of the signers of the Declaration of Independence (their births and occupations), the history of the Missouri Compromise and how the North's attempt to block the admission of Missouri shattered the "Era of Good Feelings." The paper also addressed the traditional division within the state by publishing an article about the American Revolutionary battle of Kings

Mountain, where South Carolinians fought against one another under the names "Patriots" and "Loyalists."[108]

In the winter following John C. Calhoun's death and the failures of the Nashville Convention, there was another great push for immediate and independent secession action in Georgetown. From this time forward, Georgetown was devoted to its mission to bring forth independence from the United States. The only question was if it could convince South Carolina to withdraw from the Union without the cooperation of the other slaveholding states.

Right after the passage of the Compromise of 1850, the Georgetown and All Saints Southern Rights Association announced the formation of Committees of Safety for Georgetown, Black River, Sandy Island and All Saints for defense.[109] The group resolved to move for separate state action and demanded that its senators and representatives in the legislature vote for independence. They also resolved, "That although it would be an occasion of great pleasure and satisfaction to have our sister slave holding states act in common with us, we can see no reason in their backwardness, why the State of South Carolina should fail in carrying out her declared intentions." The convention proposed that the planters, or anyone who had disposable income, invest in the program already at hand, open direct lines of trade with Europe and boycott northern trade.[110]

Following the meeting, the *Winyah Observer* published a small article titled, "Divisions of the South." The article addressed the rift in South Carolina and blamed the divisiveness between the immediate secessionists and cooperationists as the cause of most of their problems. The author stated, "Southern people, upon the subject of our own misconduct; arising from our jealousies and rivalships among one another. It is our own divisions which have enabled the Northern section of the Union to encroach upon the rights of our constitution."[111]

Chapter 4

Joshua John Ward and Robert F.W. Allston in Power

A democracy is nothing more than mob rule, where fifty-one percent of the people may take away the rights of the other forty-nine.
—Thomas Jefferson

In 1850, Georgetown and Horry Districts were well represented in the state government. That fall, All Saints Parish (Waccamaw River) rice planter Joshua John Ward took the position of lieutenant governor (Waccamaw rice planter Dr. Andrew Hasell filled his vacant seat), and Pee Dee rice planter Robert F.W. Allston retained his Senate seat representing Prince George Winyah Parish, although Allston also served the state as the president of the Senate.[112] Allston was the largest planter on the Pee Dee and Ward the largest planter on the Waccamaw. They had been working together for two decades to unite the region under the banner of separate state secession, and now the election ensured that they would work together to push the entire state toward separatism.

The new lieutenant governor, Joshua John Ward, was known as an ardent supporter of nullification and independent South Carolina secession. He started his political career as justice of the peace and justice of the quorum in Georgetown. He won two elections to the state legislature representing All Saints Parish, and beginning in 1842, the people of Georgetown and Horry Districts elected him to South Carolina's state Senate. He served in the state Senate until December 7, 1850, when he resigned to accept the lieutenant governorship of South Carolina, a position he held for one term.[113]

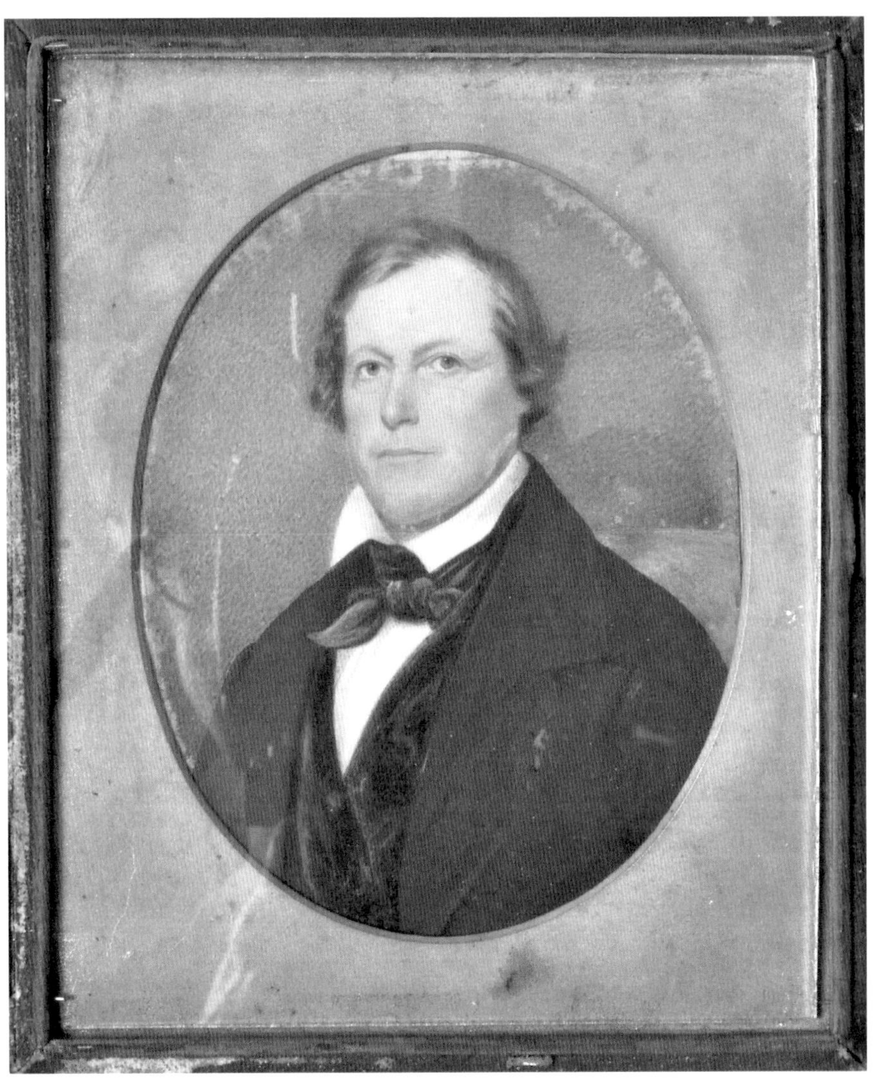

Joshua John Ward, by Charles Fraser, circa 1850. *Courtesy of Mrs. Robert L. Lumpkin. Photograph by Paige Sawyer.*

On Thursday, December 5, 1850, the Southern Rights Association of All Saints Parish formed. At the first meeting, 185 concerned citizens from Georgetown and Horry Districts assembled at the Socastee Bridge and formed the association. Dr. John D. Magill chaired the meeting. He opened the convention by reading an apology letter written by the district's most notable citizen, the Honorable South Carolina lieutenant governor Joshua

John Ward. In the letter, Ward expressed regret that his position in Columbia kept him from chairing the meeting. Next, All Saints senator Dr. Andrew Hasell gave a "spirited" address on the issue of states' rights. After pleading for unity against the central authority, preaching an embargo of trade with the northern states and defense of their homes and hearth, Hasell closed with, "We the people of All Saints Parish are ready to do our utmost in the execution of any measures defensive or offensive towards the Central Government which South Carolina our Sovereign State may adopt, and more over we will now cooperate with citizens in carrying out the system of non-intercourse with the North." On motion of Dr. Edward Thomas Heriot, the group agreed to meet twice per year—once at the Watchesaw Plantation muster field on July 4 and on December 5 at Socastee Bridge.[114]

As 1850 passed into 1851, the calls for secession and the general secession movement throughout the southern states calmed down. However, the *Winyah Observer* remained determined to rally its readers to secession by publishing several inflammatory articles. One article, "The Policy of the South," trumpeted that the South had lost its equality of power with the North and warned that although they were experiencing a temporary lull in the unfriendliness between the sections, "the hostility is increasing and inequality is increasing." The paper warned, "The political subordination of the South accomplished as it has been by spoliation, leaves her but two alternatives—redress or submission."[115]

Over the next few months, the newspaper attempted to promote South Carolina nationalism by keeping its readers informed of the glorious history of South Carolina and promoting service to the state. The paper published articles on the American Revolutionary Battle of Cowpens and an article titled, "The First Secession of South Carolina," explaining the heroic actions of South Carolinians during the American Revolution. As they did in the past, South Carolinians were being prepared to protect their rights and secure their liberties. In April, the paper printed an article in reaction to the work of the Underground Railroad in which it claimed that the "[p]eople of South Carolina are ready for secession—only strict adherence to the fugitive slave law can prevent it."[116]

As the spring of 1851 turned to summer, Georgetown and many people from Horry continued to call for secession, but the state continued to lean toward cooperation with the Union in order to stall for time to gather the support of the other southern states and to inspire foreign sympathies. In May, a southern rights convention assembled in Charleston. Despite some very strong secession talk from Georgetown and Beaufort planters, the

Charleston Convention called for moderation. The attendees concluded, "It is admitted by the most incorrigible submissionists that we have suffered injury and insult and robbery, but they call upon us to wait a while longer—wait until all of the Southern states shall be moved to resist the General Government."[117] Again, Georgetown had to swallow its pride and wait for the rest of the state to act.

On the Fourth of July, more than 150 people assembled at the Pee Dee muster field to celebrate patriotism and United States' independence from Great Britain, but along the way, the rhetoric turned from a celebration of American independence to a call for Southern Nationalism. At noon, Reverend Mr. Johnson gave an opening prayer, and George G. Ford read the Declaration of Independence. Benjamin Henry Wilson gave an hour-long oration explaining the sufferings and sacrifice of the people under the English system, which he paralleled to the utter disregard of the United States Constitution by the northern states, along with "the robbery and plunder to which one section of the Union has been subjected." He discussed the wrongs and injuries that the South had suffered and advocated South Carolina's independent secession. Addressing those who continuously called for moderation and cooperation with the other southern states, he said that he has "watched and waited until the very sentinels have fallen asleep on the towers, and had waited until the enemy was on our very threshold." A reporter in the crowd said that Wilson's sentiments were shared by about 90 percent of those in attendance.

Several toasts were given—such as from the current militia colonel and Prince George Winyah representative John Harleston Read Jr., who said, "Friends of '76 and the present; Epochs characterized by a like struggle between the spirit of liberty and oppression." Dr. James Ritchie Sparkman gave a few remarks following Read's statement, concluding with, "Her sons [South Carolina] when volunteers are called for, may not one of them be found on the fence." Prince George's Winyah senator Robert F.W. Allston, a previous gallant militia leader, turned to the Wee Nee Dragoons and said, "May they soon be resuscitated and be reanimated at the service of the State."[118] The leaders of Georgetown were promoting secession, and the people happily followed suit.

Throughout the late summer and fall of 1851, the *Winyah Observer* continued to lead the charge for secession. In an attempt to further incite its readers, the paper continuously referred to the United States' soldiers stationed in Charleston Harbor as "the Army of Occupation." It also reported that the seated president Millard Fillmore's administration was plotting to move against them. The paper flaunted South Carolina's justification for secession and promised its readers that they were honoring their American Revolution–era ancestors by declaring independence from the United States but also claimed that President Fillmore "through its leading organs, has, again, and again, threatened that the sovereign act of the state seceding from the Union, would be met by the military repression of the government."[119]

In early October, one week before a scheduled secession meeting, the newspaper printed an article titled, "The Right of Secession," printing the Virginia and Kentucky resolutions to further support the cause. The paper again called for the state to secede without the support of the other southern states and noted South Carolina's weakness in waiting for other states to heed the call. The paper claimed that this was a new day of age and complained that cooperationists always lean on John C. Calhoun—who, rightfully so, always sought compromise—but the times had changed and the people must defend their rights by seceding.[120]

On Wednesday, October 8, 1851, the Southern Rights Association of Georgetown held a meeting for the people of Georgetown and Williamsburg Districts. They met at Morris's Ferry at 11:00 a.m. to discuss secession. More than seven hundred people spread out under the lofty limbs of massive live oaks for a "Great Secession Demonstration." It was the largest meeting ever recorded in the Georgetown District. Reverend G.R. Talley opened the meeting with prayer, followed by Robert F.W. Allston, who then explained the reason for assembly: secession—not *if* they should secede, but *when* was the right time. Many ranking citizens gave speeches on what they expected the district to do. Eleazer Waterman Sr., newspaper mogul and leading voice for the cooperationists, said, "Separate state action is an error, and will not be tolerated by this meeting." Although he was a respected journalist and longtime Georgetonian who had always spoken for cooperation with the other southern states, he was clearly in the minority. Following Waterman, Mr. Samuel Taylor Atkinson rose immediately and spoke for almost an hour with "much force and ingenuity."[121]

Immediately following Atkinson, the Honorable J.L. Middleton spoke for more than an hour explaining in "his clear and lucid style, with an imagination full of historical resources, the need for immediate action." He concluded by asking the audience to move to the right of the stage if they were for immediate action and to the left of the stage if they wished to wait for the cooperation of the other southern states. The tally was taken—more than four hundred moved to the right of the stage, and only fifteen individuals moved to the left of the stage. After the vote, the entire crowd ate barbecue and enjoyed drinks at a cost of more than $1,000 to the association.[122]

By the 1850s, the sentiments of secession and patriotism had become identical to the people of Georgetown, South Carolina, as they no longer held their allegiance to the United States. In another obvious attempt to spur on Southern Nationalism, the *Winyah Observer* filled its pages with articles on South Carolinians such as Francis Marion, southern heroes such as Patrick Henry and victorious military exploits of the South such as the Battle of New Orleans.[123] It also supplied articles such as "What Constitutes Citizenship?" in which the newspaper reminded its readers that in the United States Constitution, different groups of people were listed and designated respectively: "citizens," "free persons," "Indians" and "other persons."[124] As if to say, "Love it or leave it," the newspaper also published an article titled, "The Age of Can't." In that commentary, the *Winyah Observer* recounted a *New York Times* piece that highlighted southern slave owners who opposed slavery but were forced to maintain their slaves due to strict manumission laws. The *Winyah Observer* offered the solution to southerners who were swept up in the frenzy of reform and did not submit to the social culture of the South: "We wish every White man in the South who is a slaveholder, and yet opposed to slavery, would move out of it."[125]

In late April 1852, Thomas Pinckney Alston attended a meeting of the Southern Rights Convention in Charleston that once again entertained secession. After strong debate, cooperationists defeated the secessionists. The assembly gave the legislature the power to secede if necessary but felt that the time was still not right and that they should wait and secede in cooperation with the rest of the South. Again Georgetown and other Lowcountry planters called for secession, while upcountry farmers and Charleston merchants cautioned for moderation.[126]

The presidential election in November 1852 of "Doughface" northern Democrat Franklin Pierce brought tranquility to the country and temporarily calmed South Carolina from secession. Lowcountry planters were almost all Democrats of the Thomas Jefferson variety. The Jeffersonian Democrats believed in strong states' rights and a weak Congress that did not possess the authority to enforce tariffs and create banks. Having their candidate elected (Pierce carried twenty-seven of the thirty-one states in the country), the local citizens must have been ecstatic, as it appeared that radical abolitionism and Free Soil had been beaten democratically at the polls. Whig candidate and Mexican-American War hero General Winfield Scott carried the four states that Pierce did not control. The traditional

Whig platform included protective tariffs, a national bank and distribution of federal lands. The Free Soil Party did not win any states in the election.[127]

By the election of 1852, the Great Triumvirate of Daniel Webster, John C. Calhoun and Henry Clay had all died. The three men who, as senators from Massachusetts, South Carolina and Kentucky, respectively, had argued for their sections were now all gone. The leaders of the second generation of American politicians gave way to a new breed of politicians who were tempered by their arguments but not as interested in compromise.

One month later, the *Winyah Observer* announced that Richard Dozier, Eleazer Waterman Jr. and J.W. Tarbox had purchased the *True Republican* (a paper that only had one year of circulation in Georgetown) and combined it with the *Winyah Observer* to create the *Pee Dee Times*.[128] Cooperationist Benjamin Henry Wilson was the editor of the *Winyah Observer*. With Richard Dozier as editor of the *Pee Dee Times*, the new paper proved to be far more radical than the *Winyah Observer*. The *Pee Dee Times* started in early 1853 with the maxim "Devoted to Southern Rights, Morality, Agriculture, Literature, Science, Arts and Misc" sprawled across its masthead, followed by the subheading, "If thou hast truth to utter, speak and leave the rest to God." The center column article of the first issue offered a very patriotic and defensive editorial that explained "[w]hat makes South Carolina so Great." The new newspaper proved to be far more radical than the previous newspaper. By April of the following year, Waterman had sold his share of the newspaper to the other partners, as the tabloid's rhetoric had become, perhaps, too strong for his cooperationist stance.[129]

One of the major topics explored in the early editions of the *Pee Dee Times* was the issue of combatting the abolitionists and the promoters of change in the North and West, found in articles such as "Can an Abolitionist be a Gentleman," numerous articles on their perspective of benevolent "charity" and "philanthropy" and reproachful articles on fanaticism, such as "New York Conventions."

In the article "New York Conventions," the paper indicted New York as the new leader in the various reform movements: "The Empire State has distinguished itself for holding conventions of every stripe and color—Women's rights, Greeleyite, anti-Christ, temperance, abolitionist and political." Another article played on the fears of the people by warning of "More Abolitionist Outrages" and decreeing that the North was full of fanatics who will injure those southerners who travel outside of the South: "It is now a settled matter that Southern citizens going into the Free States are considered fit game for robbery and assassination."[130]

On May 11, 1853, less than a year after the publication of Harriet Beecher Stowe's book *Uncle Tom's Cabin*, the newspaper published an article on "Harriet Beecher Stowe's Charity" in which it exposed her lack of philanthropic concern for slaves. The article described a story of a slave owner in Virginia who recently contacted a benevolent society in Philadelphia explaining that he would like to sell thirty slaves into freedom. He asked if the society could help him by raising funds necessary to free them since he had a mortgage on the chattel property. Stowe and other leading abolitionists were contacted by the benign society to help raise money for the cause. Some people contributed to the fund; however, Stowe did not offer any financial support. Instead of helping to finance the effort, apparently she returned a "sweet sympathy card with the charity of advice and approval, but no money." The *Pee Dee Times* chastised Mrs. Stowe for her lack of financial support by stating, "Her mission is to make money out of Negro philanthropy and not for it."[131]

Another inflammatory article concerning abolitionists was titled, "Condition of the Colored Population of the North," which informed citizens that they were not only lawful in keeping slaves under the Constitution but also doing God's duty by keeping their slaves in good health. The article described the free persons of color in the North as living in abject poverty, "half-starved and left to die in the gutter." The tabloid explained the actions of the abolitionists as self-serving and non-philanthropic. The newspaper complained that "the illustrations of their own directions are the very reverse of their preaching" and once again accused abolitionists of not living up to their preaching, dismissing their actions as "an example of the difference between the profession and the practice of abolition."[132]

By late 1853, the Lowcountry's interpretation of slavery had changed again. As the collective mentality shifted from the "humanitarian idealism" of Jefferson to the "economic realism" of Calhoun by the mid-1820s, the rhetoric of the mid-1850s turned to a defense of slavery as a positive good. According to the Lowcountry's new stance on slavery, all persons—slaves, masters and non-slaveholding persons—had a vested interest in seeing slavery defended and upheld.[133] One citizen of Georgetown explained that slavery was not a perfect situation and that "[t]here were cruel masters, just as there are cruel fathers, and hardheaded overseers in the mills and factories North and East, but the comforts of well-treated Negroes far surpassed those of the best regulated factories."[134]

One South Carolina politician later explained his state's view comparing immigrant hirelings and the treatment and welfare of African slaves. "The

Senator from New York said yesterday that the whole world had abolished slavery. Aye, the name, but not the thing; all the powers on Earth cannot abolish that." Later, he compared southern slaves to northern hirelings and said, "Yours are hired by the day, not cared for, and scantily compensated, which may be proved in the most painful manner, at any hour in any street in any of your large towns. Why, you meet more beggars in one day, in any single street of the city of New York, than you would meet in a lifetime in the whole South."[135]

In February 1854, the *Pee Dee Times* reprinted an article from the *New Orleans Bee* about a female slave who went to France with her mistress. Under French influence, the female servant ran away. According to the story, after a short time, the slave became frustrated by living on her own and missed being a slave, where her housing, food, clothing and medical attention were seen to by her master and mistress. Over the course of a few years, the runaway saved her money and later bought a ticket on a steamship bound for New Orleans. Once back in the South, she sought out her mistress, apologized for running away and begged to become her slave again.[136] Another article, "Northern Negro Life as Seen through a Southern Slave's Spectacles," explained an Alabama slave's trip up north with his master. The slave reported that blacks lived in complete poverty in the northern states. He reported that maids made four dollars per month at hotels and men made up to eight dollars per month. He furthered his denunciations against the northerners by claiming that most northern blacks were forced to take charity because work is hard to get due to discrimination.[137]

Secessionist extremists (referred to as "Fire-Eaters") filled the newspaper with rhetoric and waited for the next opportunity to lead the state to secession. They did not have to wait long. On May 30, 1854, the Kansas-Nebraska Act (introduced to the Senate by Stephen A. Douglas of Illinois and Andrew Butler of South Carolina) repealed the Missouri Compromise and introduced popular sovereignty into the remaining unsettled parts of the Louisiana Purchase, land that was previously divided into free and slave territories. Seeing trouble on the horizon, Richard Dozier of the *Pee Dee Times* wrote, "The bill organizing the territory of Nebraska has again waked the demon of fanaticism from the fitful and feverish slumber."[138]

On the Fourth of July 1854, about 130 people assembled at the Pee Dee muster field for the seventy-fifth anniversary of the Declaration of Independence. After the reading of the document, community leaders offered thirteen toasts, one for each colony united in the struggle for American independence. After several toasts were offered Benjamin

Henry Wilson, a partner in law with Richard Dozier and a rising Prince George Winyah politician, offered his toast. Wilson was known as a cooperationist up until that time, but with the political climate changing, he advocated "separate State secession as the most practicable and, at present, the only remedy for our grievances." He blamed "the utter disregard by the North of the Constitution, and the robbery and plunder to which one section of the Union has been subjected" as the causes for all of the indifferences between the regions, and his evolution from pursuing the cause of only seceding with the help of the other southern states, to seeking independent action.[139]

Three days later, the newspaper printed "More of the Fourth." The article centered on the dinner party following the day's celebration at the Pee Dee muster field. One of the regular toasts offered gives a clear understanding of the planters' interpretation of the authority of the federal government as it compared to states' rights. The orator declared the United States as "[a] federal compact between Sovereign States in which the Sovereignty rests not in the General Government, but in the states partied to the compact." Another toast pertained to the largest internal improvement project underway in the district, the Sampit and Santee Canal: "Although like every other enterprise, there are difficulties in the way of its construction yet if the people of Georgetown do their duty it will and shall be accomplished." The newspaper said that this toast was received with "loud and deafening applause, by about 300 persons who were present." The last toast was to Robert F.W. Allston himself for his "long and faithful service in the Senate." Allston, who presided over the dinner, delivered a few kind remarks of gratitude and sat down "amidst cheers long and loud, and congratulations of his numerous friends."[140]

In November 1854, in another attempt to rally the masses against the abolitionists, the paper ran a two-part series deflecting the South's responsibility in the slave trade. In the article "Who Were the Slave Traders," the newspaper pointed out that the New England shippers were responsible for the slave trade and reminded its readers that southerners were farmers, not seafaring people, and had no way to obtain slaves without the help of northern dealers.[141]

The *Pee Dee Times* continued to play on its readers' fears and convince them to rise to the defense of southern culture. One article, "Abolition of Negro Slavery—Its Results in the British Colonies," offered a glimpse of what could happen if slaves were set free. The journal reported that British abolitionists declared that with abolition, Jamaica would become a Garden of Eden. The newspaper blamed the abolitionists for turning Jamaica into a "waste, howling wilderness." The account explained how the exports from Jamaica were once vast but that, within a generation of abolition in the country (England banned slavery in 1833), it had become "an economic desert."[142]

In 1855, the *Pee Dee Times* announced a whole new secession problem in the United States in an article titled, "New Schemes of Disunion." The paper exposed a plan for the formation of a new republic of ten states to be carved out of states and territories of the United States. According to the plan, three new states were to be carved out of California, three out of Oregon, two out of Washington territory and two from New Mexico territory. The United States was falling apart at the seams.[143] Although concerned with the formation of a new republic out of American lands, the local people were more concerned about the developments in Kansas and "popular sovereignty."

Popular sovereignty was a noble expression in grass-roots Democracy, but when settlers in Kansas began to kill one another over the issue of slavery and an actual civil war broke out in Kansas, the phrase "Bleeding Kansas" came to life. In reaction to the trouble in Kansas, former northern Whigs, abolitionists and Free Soilists (people who were against the expansion of slavery in the West but not committed to ending slavery in the South) formed their own political party, the Republican Party.

Kansas escalated the sectional crisis to an entirely new level. Six months before violence broke out in Kansas the *Pee Dee Times* announced "The Rising Trouble in Kansas" and further warned that Missouri (as well as Kansas) could erupt into open warfare.[144] One month after the first violent clash took place in Kansas, an article titled "Kansas," written by "A Rice Planter," exclaimed, "The time of collision between slavery and abolition is near and that the point of contact must be Kansas." After explaining why southerners must take a stand in Kansas against radical abolitionists, the author wrote that he was planning to assist in any way that he could to see that Kansas entered the Union as a slave state because "I have something to lose and I do not wish to lose it, and I desire to die as I have lived."[145] Fanning the flames of war, the *Pee Dee Times* printed an article titled, "How Changed," in which it noted that "[t]he same spirit that for a sufficient reason caused it to rise against a mother, now for a more sufficient reason causes it to rise against brethren."[146] In another article printed in the same edition, Richard Dozier wrote about thirteen brothers who freed themselves from England and concluded that "now some of the brothers act like England in enforcing their will."[147] A follow-up article a few weeks later advised southern businessmen not to travel to the North in fear for their safety. "They cannot travel anywhere in the hireling States as gentlemen attended by their body servants without being mobbed and plundered."[148]

Kansas was a call to arms, and a war of words between the northern and southern press prepared both sides for action. Some Free Soil journals boasted that "the South can easily be defeated in event of Civil War." However, the *Pee Dee Times* reassured its readers that the South had at least three distinct advantages over the North. First of all, the South had slaves to work the fields. Secondly, any war fought between North and South would be fought on southern soil, where they simply had to defend themselves, not conquer to reach a peace. Lastly, the newspaper recalled that the South was more military-minded. In the Mexican-American War, of the 68,697 Americans who volunteered to fight, 45,649 came from the South, while the North only contributed 23,048. The journal pushed its readers to join in the fight to preserve their southern culture by saying, "To defend our homes—every man from 12 to 70 would volunteer to defend his home."[149]

In February 1856, local planters threw down the gauntlet and took the offensive by beginning plans for migration to Kansas. The strategy called for raising a militia of men eighteen years of age or older to move to Kansas to make sure that the state joined the country as a slave state. The paper stated that without Kansas and slavery, "free negrodom" will soon "crush out cattle, cotton, colleges, property and progress—drones will eat up the hives, railroads disappear, and the wild beasts, briners and bramblers over run the world."[150]

On February 29, 1856, perhaps motivated by the newspaper article printed two weeks earlier, concerned citizens of All Saints Parish met at the Hot and Hot Fish Club clubhouse. Dr. Andrew Hasell presided over the event, in which he organized and created a four-man committee consisting of Daniel W. Jordan, Plowden C.J. Weston, John LaBruce and Charles Alston Jr., to raise men and money to help fund the proslavery militia in their war in Kansas. The group raised $2,000 and a few volunteer troops at the meeting. John Rutledge Alston was elected to lead the pioneers to Kansas and appropriate the money raised.[151]

In its following edition, the *Pee Dee Times* screamed out, "It is the duty of the Southern States to encourage and promote bona fide emigration to the territory in Kansas." Prince George Winyah Parish responded to the call to arms. The group gathered at the Georgetown Courthouse on March 10, 1856. Those present agreed that "it is the opinion of this meeting, the example set by our brothers and friends in All Saints in raising men and money for Kansas should be followed by the people of Winyah." The group agreed to join John Rutledge Alston's All Saints men and serve with them. The following week, the people of Williamsburg and Marion met to raise men and arms for Kansas, as well.[152] In an attempt to sway more men to join the militia heading for Kansas, and in defense of the proslavery Lecompton Constitution of Kansas, Richard Dozier explained that the territory of Kansas "presented a fertile soil and a healthy climate is fairly open to bold enterprise and honest industry, and at this time is peculiarly inviting to the people of the South, in as much as a territorial Government favorable to our institutions has been organized; and is now threatened to be destroyed by the abolitionists of the North."[153]

One planter penned a collection of letters to his adult son concerning Kansas migration. He wrote, "All Saints Parish has raised $3,000 and I suppose Winyah will do the same. I have [given] $410 to major Buford, $100 to Major Herbert and $230 here."[154] In a follow-up letter, updating the Kansas fund and recruitments in Prince George Winyah, he wrote, "Seventeen men are enrolled already, and many more are willing to go. We will send a company of 20 men with $4,000 to support them." Later on in the same missive, he said, "We are disposed to fight the battle of our rights with abolition and anti-slavery on the field of Kansas."[155]

One month later, twenty-three volunteers from Georgetown and Horry met with other volunteers recruited throughout the Lowcountry in Charleston to begin their passage to Kansas.[156] On May 14, 1856, Dr. Andrew Hasell shared a letter written to him by John Rutledge Alston, who penned the dispatch while in Chattanooga en route to Kansas. Alston explained how his entire group (comprising men from All Saints, Williamsburg and Marion) was transported from Charleston on the South Carolina railroad and then the Western and Atlantic Rail Road for free and that the Chattanooga-Nashville line, as well as hotels that they used during their layovers waiting for their connecting train, gave them very good discounts.

At that point, the North had sent 1,350 men to Kansas, while the South had sent about 1,900.[157] The stage was set for the largest gang fight in American history. After years of tough talk, civilians from the North and the South squared off in the West to control the future of the United States.

Atrocities were committed by both the Jayhawkers and red legs (antislavery men) and the boarder ruffians (proslavery men). Innocent women and children on both sides, as well as male combatants, were butchered at the Pottawatomie Massacre (led by the abolitionist John Brown) in May 1856 and the Battle of Osawatomie (led by proslavery man John W. Reid) in August 1856, as well as various locations in between. Kansas was the blood-splattered classroom, a dress rehearsal for the American Civil War.

Chapter 5

Robert F.W. Allston and Plowden C.J. Weston Forge Southern Nationalism

How soon we forget history.... Government is not reason. Government is not eloquence. It is force. And, like fire, it is a dangerous servant and a fearful master.
—George Washington

The skirmishes, battles and massacres in Kansas spilled over to the Senate chambers. Senator Charles Sumner of Massachusetts rose to his feet to deliver a scornful speech titled, "The Crime Against Kansas." In his biting discourse, Sumner blamed South Carolina senator Andrew Butler for "taking the harlot slavery" into Kansas. He contended that the civil war being fought in Kansas was blood on the hands of Butler since he was one of the two architects (along with Stephan A. Douglas of Illinois) of the Kansas-Nebraska Act, which originally divided the Nebraska Territory, opening the land up to popular sovereignty. Sumner was one of a handful of northern senators who accused the South of developing and propagating a slavocracy in America, the promotion of a democracy powered by slave labor.

Three days later, South Carolina Representative Preston Brooks (Butler's nephew), intending to vindicate his uncle's good reputation, paid Sumner a visit on the Senate floor. Sumner was seated at his desk preparing to deliver yet another contemptuous verbal assault on the South when Brooks approached. Brooks calmly walked up to Sumner, addressed the senator and told him why he was paying the visit. Exchanging the medieval lance and armor for a "gutta-percha" cane, Brooks physically attacked Sumner. The assault on the Massachusetts senator was a complete surprise to everyone in attendance, who could do nothing except sit and watch the violent episode unfold. Brooks was relentless in his assault and beat Sumner over thirty times on the head and body with his walking stick. The battering left Sumner in a pool of his own blood, surrounded by pieces of his shattered desk and scattered paperwork.

The battered Sumner was carried from the Senate floor and sent home to Massachusetts, presumably to die. However, over time, Sumner recovered from the beating and his wounds healed. Northerners complained that the attack on the senator was an act of barbarism and left Senator Sumner's seat vacant in protest. Brooks was fined $300 for his outburst and resigned his seat in the House before he could be removed. Southerners hailed the South Carolina representative and his actions as a chivalrous display of respect for the elder senator. Supporters paid his fine and sent him canes, cups and walking sticks with nametags attached to them insinuating that they wanted him to beat other congressmen.[158]

In July 1856, a group assembled at the Georgetown Post Office to discuss the Brooks-Sumner Affair. To the cavaliers of the Lowcountry, southern gentlemen were supposed to battle again and again in affairs of honor just like the medieval knights of old. As per their code of chivalry, the group stated that Brooks's actions were "not only a vindication of personal right, but a patriotic defense of South Carolina and Southern honor." The *Pee Dee Times* not only supported Brooks but also accused Sumner of acting falsely to God, country and truth. The assemblage blamed Sumner for the affair and charged him with hypocrisy, having "swore to defend the Constitution with hand on bible, but is guilty of trying to incite Civil War." The group decided to send Brooks a new cane with an inscription on it showing its approval of his action.[159] Over the next several months, Brooks went on a tour of the state, as "Brooks Dinners" were held to honor his actions and bestow gifts on him.[160]

The violence on the Senate floor was a gut-check for all politicians, North and South. One South Carolina senator wrote that "every man in both Houses is armed with a revolver—some with two—and a bowie knife. It is, I fear in the power of any Red or Black Republican to precipitate at any moment a collision in which the slaughter would be such as to shock the world and dissolve the government." Advertising his dedication to regional pride and Southern Nationalism, the senator went on to say, "I keep a pistol now in my drawer in the Senate as a matter of duty to my section."[161]

That summer and fall, articles on the South's ability to defend itself militarily from the North, along with renewed calls for secession with the

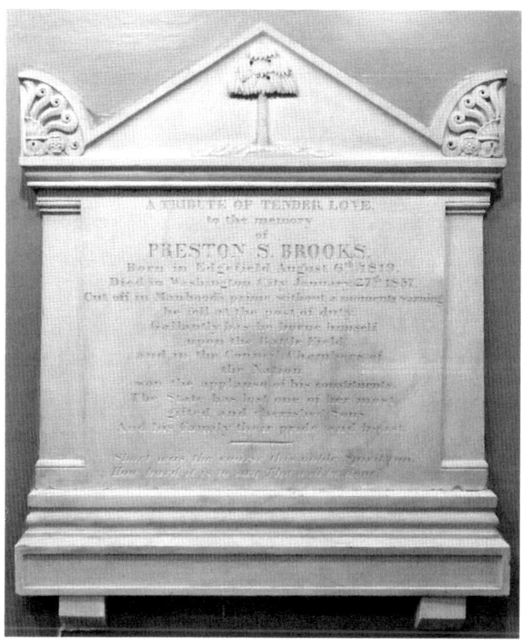

Preston S. Brooks memorial tablet, in the foyer of South Caroliniana Library. *Courtesy of the South Caroliniana Library, University of South Carolina, Columbia, South Carolina.*

formation of a "Southern Confederacy," filled the newspaper. In an obvious attempt to boost the morale of the people and unify southerners in defense of their homes and hearth, the *Pee Dee Times* bragged that no army on the planet could defeat the South—"Not the North, nor even Great Britain." The article claimed that southern traditions were worth fighting to defend and outlined a plan for defending against runaway slaves. The author appealed to the citizens to rally to the call to defend against possible invaders by saying, "The abolitionists think that they can count on the slaves to help them, but they would immediately be moved to the interior of the South and then we could easily defend the frontier."[162]

While Americans North and South debated the actions of their politicians, the *Pee Dee Times* asked its readers "What Constitutes a Gentleman"? At that time, one of the greatest compliments that could be bestowed on a man was the ceremonious title of "gentleman." After considering if gentility revolved around wealth, dress and manners, the author of the article concluded that wealth and fine clothing had nothing to do with gentility: "Gentility is not wealth; it is not in dress, nor genius, nor any other attribute of man, unless it goes hand in hand with a cheerful disposition, an amiable temper and a philanthropic will. There are real bonafide Gentlemen in all classes of society, and he is the greatest gentleman who mingles with all, and remains untarnished." Later on in the same article, the author wrote, "Real gentility is moral freedom; it respects no particular person, as a class beyond their merits; it does not exclude one man because he is poor; but embracing all who are worthy, it regards them as kindred souls who should ever dwell harmonious together. This constitutes a gentleman."[163]

The presidential election of 1856 was a powder keg that included two new political parties and the steadfast traditional Democratic Party. South Carolina's position at the Democratic National Convention was to fight for the deterioration of abolitionists' tendencies and prevent federal policies and Republican-proposed policies (e.g., the Homestead Act and protective tariff hikes) that were obviously anti-southern.[164]

The Democratic candidate James Buchanan won the election with 174 electoral votes and carried nineteen states. Although he was from Pennsylvania, he was categorized as a "Dough-faced Democrat," one from the North who had southern principles or at least sympathized with the southern region. Southerners were relieved with his victory since Buchanan promised to add Cuba to the country as a slave state and clung to southern values such as the promotion of low tariffs.[165] John C. Frémont, under the banner of the newly formed Republican Party, made a strong showing. In their first national polling, the Republicans carried eleven states and recorded 114 electoral votes.

While the Democratic Party ran a balanced platform representing all three regions (North, South and West) of the United States, the Republican Party openly and clearly identified itself as a regional political party. The Republican platform offered northern industrialists higher protective tariffs and internal improvements to the West paid for by the tariff. The Republicans also offered a Homestead Act for the developing west. The proposed Homestead Act offered a 160-acre plot of land for a family farm to anyone who filed for the land. The act effectively excluded southern planters from the West because plantations required far more land than 160 acres to turn a profit. The Republican Party offered nothing to the South. Former president Millard Fillmore carried eight electoral votes and the state of Maryland with the newly formed American Party, also known as the Know Nothing Party.

In the melee of the 1856 election season, South Carolinians elected Georgetonian Robert F.W. Allston governor. Allston had served his entire adult life in public service in preparation for the governorship. He graduated from the United States Military Academy at West Point in 1821, and in June 1821, he was commissioned lieutenant in the Third Artillery, Topographical Service, a position he held for only a few months. In 1822, he was elected

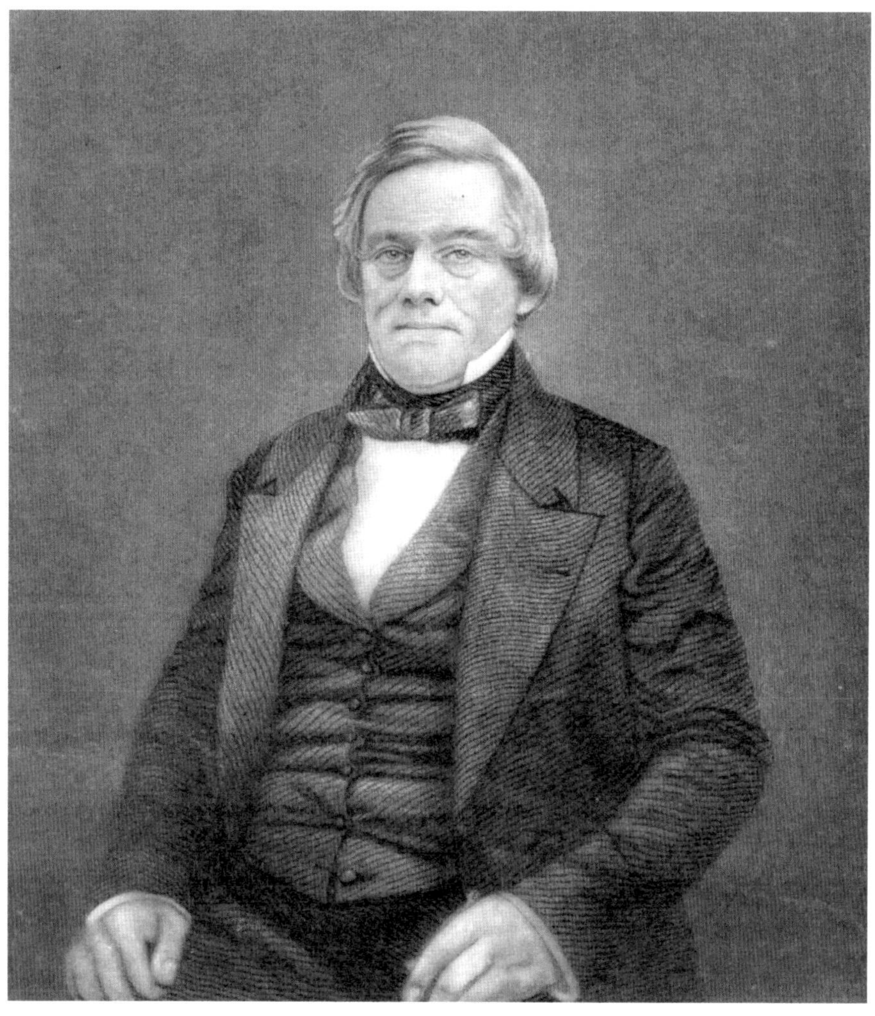

Robert Francis Withers Allston, engraved by Illman & Sons for *De Bow's Review*, New Orleans. *Courtesy of the South Caroliniana Library, University of South Carolina, Columbia, South Carolina.*

to his first public office, surveyor general of South Carolina, a position he held for two terms (four years). In 1827, he assumed the management of his estate and officially became a rice planter. The following year, Allston was elected to the South Carolina House of Representatives, where he served from 1828 to 1832.[166] In 1832, as a strong supporter of John C. Calhoun's Nullification Doctrine, Allston became the state senator from Prince George Winyah, an office he held for twenty-four years (serving as the president of the Senate from 1850 to 1856). While serving in the state Senate, Allston attended the Nashville Convention in 1850 and contributed to a fundraiser to send slaveholders to Kansas in 1856.[167] He resigned his seat in the state Senate to accept the governorship of South Carolina on December 10, 1856. Allston served one term as governor.[168]

In a missive to his son, Benjamin Allston, the year earlier, Robert F.W. Allston expressed how the notion of deference compelled planters to lead society. "It is rather probable I may be elected Govr. next year. And if elected I have promised to serve. Tho' God knows I would be better off at home. The novelty of the position and my ambition for it have long ceased, but on being appeal'd to by my constituents and by my friends of the Pee Dee Country, it would have been selfish of me to decline."[169]

The events leading up to the election of 1856 drew Waccamaw rice planter and intellectual recluse Plowden C.J. Weston out of his ten-year scholarly seclusion at his Hagley Plantation on the Waccamaw. Compelled by noblesse oblige to lead, Weston broke onto the scene with the vigor and strength of a young man and the discipline and education of an accomplished scholar. Weston had spent the previous decade living a life of scholarly isolation surrounded by his library of rare and valuable books. He burst onto the antebellum scene, contributed to the annals of history and served his state in political office.

Few southerners aspired to be authors during the antebellum period; however, Weston, the scholar-planter, had several publications. Besides composing a poem entitled "The Pleasures of Music," Weston inspired South Carolina nationalism when in 1856 he edited *Documents Connected with the History of South Carolina*, a collection of documents pertaining to the early history of South Carolina (121 copies printed).[170] Weston also wrote "The Overseer's Contract," a detailed description of the overseer's duties on a rice plantation, which *DeBow's Review* published in 1857.[171] Also in 1857, Weston published a blistering secessionist speech titled, *An Address by Plowden C.J. Weston before the Citizens of All Saints at Watchesaw Plantation, 4th July, 1857.*[172] In 1860, he published his last two works: a fire-eating oratory entitled *An Address Delivered in the Indigo Society Hall, Georgetown, South Carolina* and *The Rules and History of the Hot and Hot Fish Club of All Saints Parish*, which he edited. A lifelong student of history, Weston was instrumental in forming the South Carolina Historical Society and belonged to the Maryland and New York Historical Societies.[173]

In November 1856, Weston won the election for the All Saints District House of Representatives seat (he eventually served two terms in that body

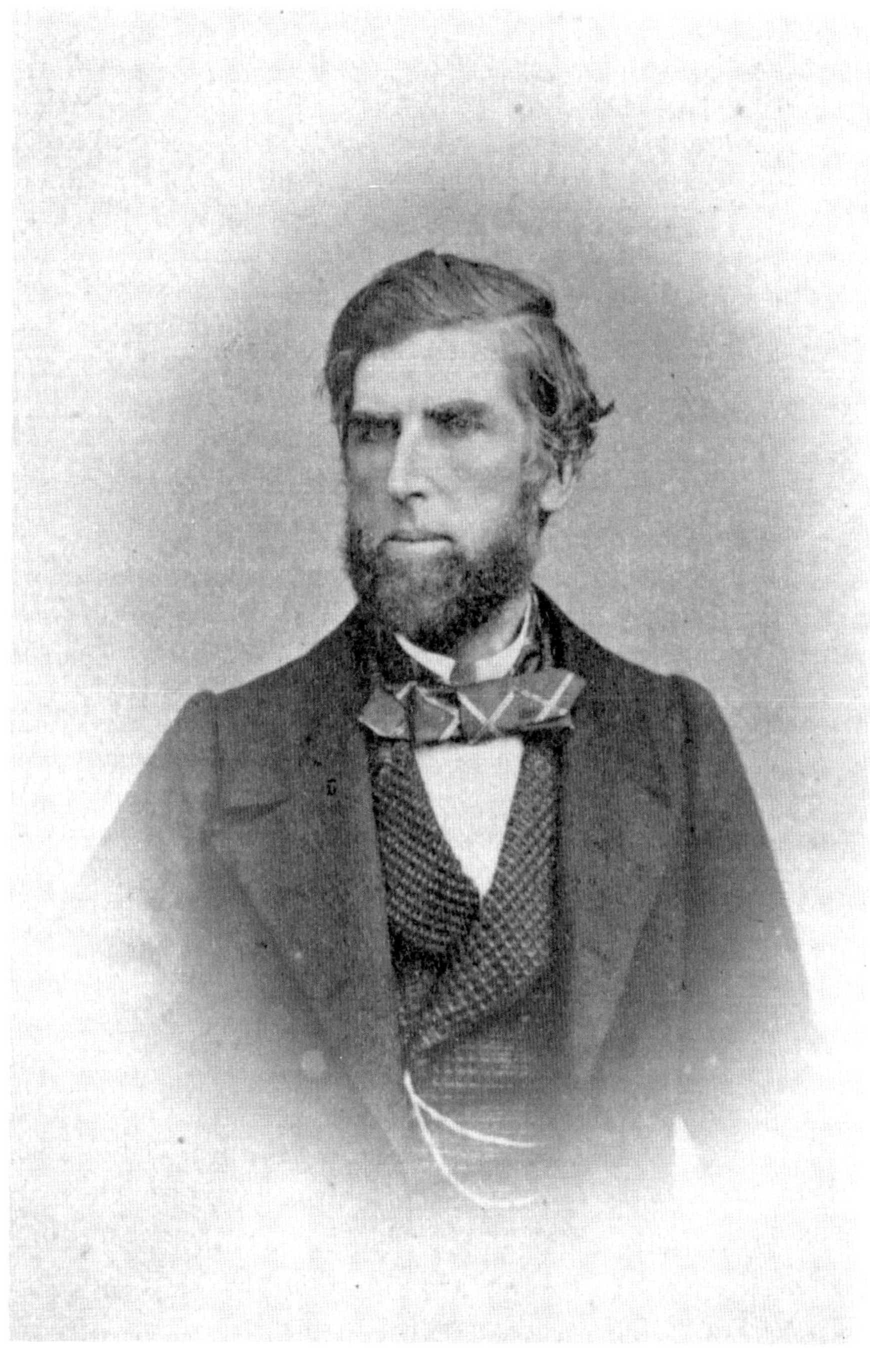

Plowden C.J. Weston. *Photo courtesy of the Confederate Museum, Charleston, South Carolina.*

and later as lieutenant governor of the state). In 1856, Allston and Weston led the secessionists' camp in Georgetown, and John Harleston Read Jr. (Prince George Winyah Parish representative from 1844 until 1861 in the general assembly) led the cooperationists' faction.[174]

On March 3, 1857, just one day before president-elect James Buchanan took office, Congress passed the tariff of 1857. The new tariff reflected the president-elect's stance on tariffs, lowering taxes on imports to 20 percent, the lowest levy on imports since the beginning of tariff collection. The act was very unpopular in the North but hailed in the South. Two days after Buchannan took the office of the presidency, and one month after Preston Brooks died from disease, the Supreme Court endorsed the principles of southern rights in the Dred Scott Decision.[175]

The conservative position in South Carolina was strengthened when U.S. Chief Justice Roger Taney announced that Dred Scott, a slave who attempted to use the Supreme Court to sue for his freedom because his master took him into free states and territories, could not use the court because he was not a citizen, but rather property. Furthermore, the court explained, the Missouri Compromise, with its 36–30 dividing line of the West between free and slave states, was unconstitutional, and the federal government did not have the power to dictate where citizens of the United States could and could not take their property. There were no longer "free" states and slave states but rather united states with slavery and without legal restraints. The *Pee Dee Times* trumpeted the ruling, "The Republican Party henceforth must choose between submission and revolution—loyalty or treason to the government."[176]

That spring, the region swelled with sectional pride, political accomplishment, optimism for the future and a feeling of general triumph. Spring always brought militia drills and parades to the area, but this time, one of their own was the governor of the state. The Thirty-First Regiment infantry paraded under review and drilled at Black Mingo on Wednesday, March 23. The Thirty-Third Regiment paraded in Conwayboro (renamed in December 1855) on Saturday, March 28, and the Thirty-Second Regiment gathered at the Marion Courthouse and paraded on Tuesday, March 31. Other drills took place at Camden, Darlington, Lancaster, Chesterfield and Marlborough. Cavalry units attended.[177]

The highlight of the spring parade season took place in Georgetown. The Thirty-First Regiment of South Carolina's militia held a general muster, with all beats reporting. This was the first general muster in several years and was newly elected governor Robert F.W. Allston's first appearance as governor in the Pee Dee. As commander in chief of South Carolina, Allston reviewed the dragoons and infantry in front of a large crowd of spectators. *Pee Dee Times* editor Richard Dozier could not contain his excitement and reported on the event with great patriotism to South Carolina: "At this time, the quill is out of vogue, and everybody has resigned himself to the glory that clusters round the sword and the plume."[178]

Blooming with martial dreams and justified by the recent Supreme Court decision, the *Pee Dee Times* published "Duty of Southern Men," a call to arms to its readers to defend their homes and firesides against the threat of invaders. Talking of the two sections of the country, as if preparing the regions for a winner-takes-all latter-day joust, the author said that indifferences between the regions took place before the slavery agitation but that "[i]t is true, that before the dawn of this insanity, our lances clashed occasionally, and that one or the other was unhorsed, but the tilt did no serious damage to the contestants." With the recent agitation, however, things seemed far more serious.[179] The mindset of the day was that "the day of apologies for slavery and compromise with abolitionism, is past."[180]

In 1857, the Fourth of July Independence Day gathering was a major event that was very well attended. The Winyah and All Saints States Rights Association sponsored the event at Watchesaw Plantation. All Saints General Assemblyman Plowden C.J. Weston accepted the invitation to speak at the patriotic event. He opened his speech by calling it the anniversary to celebrate Gadsden, Pinckney, Middleton, Rutledge and Marion. He informed the audience that there was an old Hindustan belief that the souls of deceased heroes are allowed to return to their place of life once per year on the anniversary of their greatest deed or action to listen to the living praise them. Although a devoted Christian, Weston used the Hindu faith for the opportunity to recall the deeds of past South Carolinians and rally the people to patriotism and southern nation building.[181]

During his address, Weston acknowledged the growing threat posed by the Republican Party and expressed his fear that it could gain control of the executive office of the presidency. He then recounted the culmination of the Kansas crisis and the Dred Scott case as "a crisis inferior in danger to none that those men encouraged in the Revolution." He offered an appeal to South Carolina's deceased heroes of the American Revolution: "Illustrious immortals! Doubt not we shall follow in your steps! August spirits! Think not that your children will derogate from your example."[182]

Weston called on South Carolinians to unite for war and expressed how all white southerners were equal in this coming struggle to defend agriculture and their rights from the northern majority. He explained how southerners treat one another with more respect than do northerners and said that the differences between citizens in the American South were natural ones of "education, industry, good conduct and their results—and inequality is not even supposed or pretended." He went on to say that slavery was the determiner that kept all whites equal and alleged "the smallest inequality between citizens is abominable and atrocious….[N]ot more than two-thirds of whites own slaves, yet the maintenance of authority is of equal, or of greater advantage and necessity to the non-slave holding rather than to the slave holding class. By introducing and maintaining a subordinate and inferior class, the property of the rich clothes the poor with power." Weston reaffirmed that all whites were equal as citizens and noted that the citizenry in the South was completely "contrary to the example of other nations where the separation between the rich and poor is caused by an incompatibility of interests and increases daily."[183]

An alarmist by nature, Weston gave a glimmer of hope that war with the United States could be avoided due to commercial interests: "Nothing but the absolute necessity which the world has of its being supplied with our great staples prevents a large portion of the citizens of the United States and a majority of civilized Europe from banding themselves together in an open enmity against us."[184]

Weston further defended slavery by insisting that Africans were better off in America than they were in Africa, praised Christianity for uplifting both races and insisted that the races aided each other. He held that "[c]ivilization, Christianity, and wealth go hand in hand, and both races, differing from each other in everything, except in those moral perceptions which are necessary for the definition of man, confer on each other benefits which outlast the present state of existence and shall not be terminated by the grave."[185]

Representative Weston articulated his greatest fear that the United States government would force emancipation. He stated that if slaves were to be set free, the abolitionists would not stop at their crusade. He prophesized, "With this unholy alliance between slaves and Northerners, they will make them citizens and give them voting rights and rights to hold office under the federal government and together they will out vote us on everything dear to us and take away our political rights and freedoms and keep us in complete subjugation."[186]

Weston called on the people to unite and rally to fight two more times in his lecture. He first paraphrased Thomas Paine's *The American Crisis* when he said, "The times are coming which are again to try men's souls, that is, to test the self-reliance, the courage, the energy, the attachment to liberty, and the moral dignity of every man amongst us." Later on that day, he said, "Soon will the mighty hands of destiny and opportunity meet on the dial-plate of time—then will it be our duty to take to our line firmly, to adhere inflexibly to the maintenance of those rights, won by our fathers and enlarged by ourselves, throwing aside all care of life and property, since neither are of any value when independence and freedom have departed."[187]

Like a great professor addressing his students in true Socratic fashion, Weston asked his contemporaries, friends and family at Watchesaw Plantation if they knew the definitions of the words *revolution* and *reform*. Answering his own question, Weston said, "I know that for successful agriculture a continual turning of the ground is necessary, but this would be the earthquake leveling everything that is high and crushing everything that is lowly; cleaving up deep pits where once stood fertile fields; raising desolate hills where once spread fertilizing lakes." He continued, "I know that the gentle agitation of the waves is necessary to maintain the sweetness of the sea, but this would be the awful rage of the billows when they break in thunder over some perishing wreck." He added, "I know that the breeze is necessary to freshen the face of nature and to carry commerce over the deep; but this would be the tornado bursting over Earth and ocean, sweeping down navies in their pride and mixing sea and shore in indistinguishable confusion. Shall we then call this intended change by the name of Revolution?"[188]

He ended his oration with a final rally to arms: "The defense of our country, let us firmly protect the institutions God has given us to preserve, and with settled resolutions, uphold the ancient freedom of South Carolina."[189]

On August 24, 1857, a financial panic commenced. It was the first worldwide economic crisis and the worst financial catastrophe in American history up to that time. The fiscal meltdown affected many western banks and was brought on by the declining international economy and overexpansion of the domestic economy, including overspeculation in western railroad construction. American banks followed English bankers in printing and lending out far more specie than they had in hard reserve. In many cases, American banks lent out seven dollars for every one dollar they held in gold and silver bullion. Farmers and newly unemployed industrial and internal improvement employees called for a Homestead Act, one of the key components of the Republican platform of 1856. With the financial Panic of 1857, the Republican Party drew even greater attention and vowed to make a difference in the next election.

VALUE OF SOUTH CAROLINA'S CASH CROPS IN 1857

Cash Crop	*Value of Export from the South*	*Plantations Involved in Cultivation*
cotton	$125,000,000	74,000
tobacco	$14,717,530	15,745
rice	$17,179,530	551
naval stores	$2,049,656	n/a

Published in the Pee Dee Times, *June 21, 1857.*

On November 23, 1857, Governor Robert F.W. Allston addressed the state. As if calling Plowden C.J. Weston into action and propelling him to statewide fame, Allston called for new, strong leaders to rise in South Carolina to fill the vacancies created with the recent deaths of John C. Calhoun, Langdon Cheves, Preston Brooks and Andrew Butler.[190]

Allston then addressed the financial crisis of 1857. He reassured his constituents that the banks of South Carolina were solvent. However, he sent a stern warning to the bankers by warning them "if they are dependent on the banks and brokers of New York, as to fail in their pledges to the public, when Northern banks fail, it is their misfortune to have to answer for the sins of others, well as for their own mismanagement."[191]

Next, he offered his empathy to the people of Kansas: "Our friends in Kansas, who have struggled manfully to sustain an unequal contest, are entitled to our sympathy—'tis all we have a right to offer."[192] Then Allston addressed the Dred Scott Decision and announced that Maine and Connecticut had protested against the Supreme Court decision. He applauded the Supreme Court's decision and gave a proslavery speech that was very similar to the one Weston gave in July to the people of Watchesaw Plantation. He blamed the slave trade on the English and New England shippers and then praised South Carolinians and southerners for doing God's work in Christianizing the Africans. Allston boasted that it was by the providence of God that southerners were able to "convert the barbarian bushmen of the African coast into the orderly domestic Christian black-laborers of America."[193]

During the second half of 1857, the *Pee Dee Times* published several politically charged speeches, including Weston's speech from Watchesaw Plantation and Allston's November speech.[194] Other articles were celebrations such as "Kansas Bleeds No More" or reported the opening of a railroad connection from Charleston and Savannah to Memphis, Tennessee.[195]

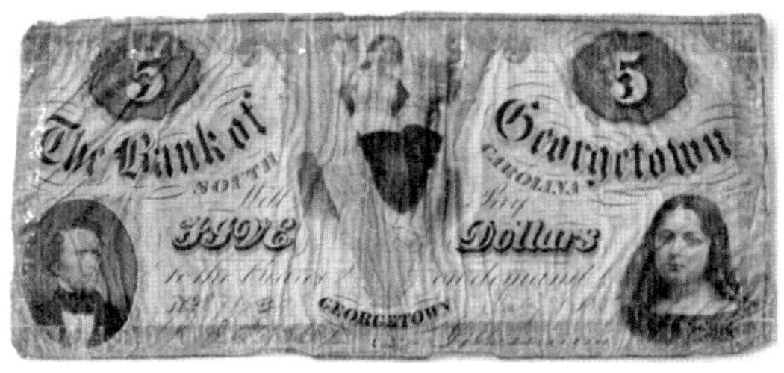

Bank of Georgetown, South Carolina. *Photo by Bob Howes.*

One article, "Life in Northern Cities," described a hateful civilization built on greed, while another, "White Slavery in Massachusetts," explained the life of industrial workers as receiving poor pay and living in almshouses. According to the article, nine out of every ten hands who are disqualified to work in the factories due to injury are sent off to the almshouses or have their labor sold in a public auction, where their work is purchased for a year. The article further accused the industrialists of abusing their employees by saying that the immigrants were worked fourteen hours per day and lived in squalor. The article ended with a poignant denunciation of the industrialists and the reformers who were quick to judge the South but unwilling to protest the problems of industrialization. The charges leveled, "What do they care for human suffering? What is their philanthropy but a fashionable excitement which they substitute for drinking liquor and smoking tobacco, because it is cheaper and more the vogue?"[196]

Chapter 6

The Bonds of the Union Unknotted

Not in hostility to others, not to injure any section of the country, not even
For our pecuniary benefit; but from the high and solemn motive of
Defending and protecting the rights we inherited and which
It is our duty to transmit unshorn to our children.
–Jefferson Davis, United States Senate, January 21, 1861

On May 4, 1858, feeling strong and defiant on the United States Senate floor, South Carolina senator James Henry Hammond explained how the southern people of the Union were the "chosen people of modern times." He pleaded at last for the creation of Southern Nationalism and for southerners to stand together to stem the tide of change. He warned those outside the South that "[w]ithout the South's cotton England would topple headlong and carry the whole civilized world with her—save the South." He furthered his argument by saying, "No, you dare not make war on cotton.… Cotton is King."[197]

Hammond delivered his "Mud-Sill" speech as a reaction to the admission of Kansas into the Union as a free state. Later on in his speech, Hammond argued about various other complaints. Another poignant argument in the speech pertained to the mismanagement and unscrupulous lending policies of the big banks. In reaction to the collapse of the Bank of England, which caused the worldwide financial Panic of 1857, Hammond said, "When the abuse of credit had destroyed credit and annihilated confidence; when thousands of the strongest commercial houses in the world were coming down, and hundreds of millions of dollars of supposed property evaporating in thin air; when you came to a dead lock, and revolutions were threatened, what brought you up? Fortunately for you it was the commencement of the cotton season, and we have poured in upon you one million six hundred thousand bales of cotton just at the crisis to save you from destruction."[198]

During that same month, representatives from throughout the South met at the Southern Commercial Convention in Montgomery, Alabama. The main topics discussed were the enforcement of the federal Fugitive Slave Law (which was not being enforced to their approval), how to deal with labor shortages since the slave trade was closed (apprenticeships and the importation of free blacks were discussed), the tariff, the further development of southern agricultural industry (internal improvements and steamers to carry staples to market), the expansion of southern libraries, schools and colleges and the relationship between the federal government and the southern states as it pertained to expansion (the question was if new territories were going to be evenly divided between the North and the South).[199] It is clear to see that the southern states were developing Southern Nationalism by coming together as a voting bloc due to their shared economic, social and political interests. At the same time, they were leaving themselves wiggle room to be able to remain part of the United States.

With American Independence Day quickly approaching, the *Pee Dee Times* published an article explaining the beliefs and opinions of many locals concerning the celebration of the birth of the United States. The paper stated that many readers "would rather celebrate the anniversary of a Southern Confederacy, than the declaration of our independence that was. But as long as we are in the Union let us not be wanting in celebrating the valorous deeds of our ancestors—the independence they achieved, had we the courage to maintain it."[200]

On July 7, 1858, Richard Dozier of the *Pee Dee Times* painted a grim picture for his readers of the state of the Union, as seen through the events of the Fourth of July celebration. He reported that the anniversary of the birthday of the United States passed "quietly and pleasantly, but with little of that public demonstration usual on such occasion." He noted that the day was ushered in with the roar of artillery and church bells ringing early in the morning, but he stated that the day did not feature a reading of the Declaration of Independence, any patriotic speakers or parades. Dozier attributed the lackluster celebration to the sectional crisis, stating that "house divided in itself, which at no distant day its splendid edifice must crumble in the dust." He wrote that the day was a pleasant ninety-one degrees with a light breeze and that a few flags were displayed in "conspicuous places" in Georgetown.[201]

There were few official events taking place to report. There was a great regatta of four miles that began at 3:00 p.m. from the Market (clock tower) and concluded at the Pilot House. The four-mile race lasted less than forty minutes. The Hook and Ladder Company hosted a shooting contest in town and awarded prizes to the best shots. Other than those two events, the weary town of Georgetown, incensed from the long economic, political and social contest between the regions, preferred to defiantly spend the day quietly reflecting on the deeds of past generations and not focusing on the present conundrums.[202]

Few issues of the *Pee Dee Times* newspaper survive after July 1858. In May 1859, the *Times* ceased publication. Richard Dozier, by then the sole proprietor of the newspaper, closed the doors of operation and focused on his political career. He was elected to replace John Izard Middleton in the state General Assembly in 1857 and qualified on December 12, 1857. He held his seat through the 1861 sessions.

On October 16, 1859, John Brown (a veteran of the civil war in Kansas) raided a federal arsenal in Harpers Ferry, Virginia. Brown planned to take over the arsenal and steal weapons and advocated a slave rebellion to kill slaveholders, their wives and children in Virginia. He and his followers easily took over the arsenal but failed to distribute the weapons, and slaves did not rise up to kill their masters. Instead, a detachment of federal troops recaptured the arsenal on October 18 and arrested Brown and his supporters. Brown was hanged less than two months later and quickly became a martyr to the abolitionist cause. With tensions rising, and fear of John Brown copycats, South Carolina immediately allocated $100,000 for military preparations, and men throughout the state began drilling and preparing for defense. After years of attempting to promote Southern Nationalism and cooperation among the southern states, it was the radical abolitionist John Brown who unified South Carolina.[203]

Jacob Motte Alston recalled John Brown's raid and gave insight into the planters' view of the abolitionists. He said, "Was there any justice when instead of 'insuring domestic tranquility,' the abolitionists of the North and East left no stone unturned to stir up strife among our servants and incite them into insurrection, and subsequently to have marched into Virginia with the avowed purpose of murdering the whites and freeing the slaves, as John Brown and his band attempted?" Alston later asked himself in his diary, "If this is the letter and the spirit of the Constitution then were the Southern States most unwise, to use a mild term, to enter into any such compact?"[204]

Between the sudden changes in social habits and the massive push toward industrialization, it seemed to the planters that their entire world was unraveling. In the years since open warfare commenced in Kansas, a transatlantic cable connected North America to Europe; Pony Express riders carried the United States mail from St. Louis, Missouri, to San Francisco, California, in ten days or less; telegraph cables linked the East and, soon, would cross the continent; and more than thirty thousand miles of railroad crisscrossed the United States (in 1830, there were only forty miles of railroad track in the United States).

In the North, more than 140,000 factories employed more than 1.5 million employees (mostly women and children). Immigrants from Ireland and the German states poured into the northeastern cities, which already teemed with unskilled labor. The huddled masses packed into tenement houses with poor sanitation and ventilation and, without sewage systems, suffered from diseases spread by rat and insect infestations. Outside, the high rise dwellings and dimly lit streets shadowed soaring crime rates as assorted criminals roamed the streets and gangs fought for turf in the overcrowded ghettos. Dirt roads, piled high with trash, were clogged with street vendors, unemployed mobs of men and animal-drawn carts, dead animals, meat cuttings and entrails from butcher shops and human and animal waste. Thomas Jefferson's prophetic warning to steer clear of industry for fear of becoming as corrupt and polluted as Europe had seemingly come to fruition.

In November 1859, Charles Darwin's book *On the Origins of Species by Means of Natural Selection* was published. In the work, Darwin proposed that populations change to adapt to their environments and, ultimately, form new species. This groundbreaking work on evolution was, undoubtedly, seen as yet another offense to the planter class, who held dear to traditionally held Christian values. This infraction against Christianity, coupled with the musical rendition (essentially minstrel shows) of the traveling Tom Shows (theatrical productions of Harriet Beecher Stowe's book *Uncle Tom's Cabin*), infuriated planters, who saw them as continued assaults on their civilization.

In April 1860, Charleston held the Democratic Party Convention. The party split along sectional lines forming two parties when Mississippi and Alabama—followed by South Carolina, Florida, Georgia, Louisiana and Texas—walked out in protest. The Democratic Party split again when John Bell led a group of former northern Whigs and former Know Nothings in the formation of the Constitutional Union Party. The party refused to take a position on slavery except to declare that it was legal in the United

States Constitution. In June, southerners met in Richmond and nominated John C. Breckinridge, the seated vice president of the United States under President James Buchanan, and northern Democrats chose Stephen A. Douglas as their standard bearer at the Baltimore Convention. The last national party officially splintered, and it would prove impossible for the regions to come together on political compromise. The die was cast—the stage was set for civil war. Like England in the mid-1600s, Cavaliers and Puritans once again prepared for war.

Throughout South Carolina history, its politicians have threatened to leave the United States and assert their independence as their state increasingly lost influence in national politics to the northern seaboard states. When Abraham Lincoln won the presidential election in November 1860 without winning a single electoral vote from the South, South Carolina felt compelled to act. The *Charleston Mercury* screamed out, "The Tea has been thrown overboard—the revolution of 1860 has been initiated." The newspaper called for "minutemen," militias and slave patrols throughout the state to prepare for war.[205] A few days later, on November 13, 1860, the South Carolina General Assembly in joint session ratified an act calling for a "Convention of the People to Convene in Columbia on December 17."

Elections for delegates to the convention took place on December 6, 1860. Each district in South Carolina sent representatives to assemble and discuss secession. Georgetown and Horry sent eight representatives. Attorney Samuel Taylor Atkinson and rice planters Judge Benjamin Faneuil Dunkin, Dr. Alexius Mador Forster and Dr. Francis S. Parker represented Prince George Winyah. Benjamin E. Sessions and rice planter John Izard Middleton represented All Saints Parish, and Kingston Parish sent attorney and merchant Thomas Beaty and William J. Ellis.[206]

Collectively, 169 men attended the convention, which convened on the previously proposed date. Most were planters, but some came from all other professions as well, including slaveless farmers, manufacturers, attorneys, judges, physicians, professors, clergymen, merchants, brokers, solicitors, the president of a railroad, the president of an insurance company and even a schoolteacher who owned neither slaves nor property in South Carolina.[207]

On December 20, 1860, the representatives signed the Ordinance of Secession, officially withdrawing South Carolina from the Union. A breakout group at the convention, operating under the name the 1860 Association, formed to facilitate a call to arms. Robert Newman Gourdin, chairman of the 1860 Association, wrote letters to notable men throughout South Carolina requesting them to do all that they could to support the newly

The State of South Carolina.

At a Convention of the People of the State of South Carolina, begun and holden at Columbia on the Seventeenth day of December in the year of our Lord one thousand eight hundred and sixty, and thence continued by adjournment to Charleston, and there by divers adjournments to the Twentieth day of December in the same year —

An Ordinance To dissolve the Union between the State of South Carolina and other States united with her under the compact entitled "The Constitution of the United States of America."

We, the People of the State of South Carolina, in Convention assembled, do declare and ordain, and it is hereby declared and ordained, That the Ordinance adopted by us in Convention on the twenty third day of May in the year of our Lord one thousand seven hundred and eighty eight, whereby the Constitution of the United States of America was ratified, and also all Acts and parts of Acts of the General Assembly of this State, ratifying amendments of the said Constitution, are hereby repealed; and that the union now subsisting between South Carolina and other States, under the name of "The United States of America," is hereby dissolved.

Done at Charleston the twentieth day of December, in the year of our Lord one thousand eight hundred and sixty.

D. F. Jamison Delegate from Barnwell and President of the Convention.

Attest Benj. F. Arthur Clerk of the Convention

South Carolina's Ordinance of Secession. *Courtesy of South Carolina History and Archives.*

established South Carolina nation. His private letters served a threefold purpose: first, as his letters were individualized, to more privately attempt to explain the impending crisis; second, to prepare, print and distribute pamphlets and other literature to "urge the necessity of resisting Northern and federal aggression"; and lastly, to set up military organization for South Carolina.[208] Shortly thereafter, the 1860 Winyah Association formed to help support the larger association to meet its goals.[209]

Robert Barnwell Rhett was charged with heading a committee to write an appeal to the other southern states asking for their cooperation in creating a Southern Confederacy. He penned *Address of the People of South Carolina, Assembled in Convention, to the People of the Slaveholding States of the United States.* Rhett's central argument was the right of self-government. He accused the North of having the desire to control the South and focused on the struggle to maintain a free government. He also explained how the North and South had grown apart and were no longer held together with a spirit of goodwill and brotherly veneration and should, therefore, separate in peace.

He explained how, in his belief, the government of the United States was "no longer the Government of Confederated Republics, but of a consolidated Democracy." He claimed that the government was "no longer a free government, but despotism," and likened the central government of the United States to the central authority of Great Britain, which "was resisted and defeated by a seven years struggle for independence." He reminded his readers that the American Revolution was fought for the great principles of "self-government and self-taxation, the criterion of self-government," and that without the protection of those principles "the southern states, are compelled to meet the very despotism, their fathers threw off in the Revolution of 1776."[210]

Rhett further explained in his treatise that there was no difference between taxation without any representation and taxation without a representation adequate to protection. He illustrated that southerners were the minority in Congress and, as a result, would not be able to defend their region from unjust taxation. He further explained how the South is taxed by the people of the North for their benefit exactly in the way that Great Britain taxed the colonies in the 1700s. Rhett said, "The people of the South have been taxed by duties on imports, not for revenue, but for an object inconsistent with revenue—to promote, by prohibitions, Northern interests in the productions of their mines and manufacturers."[211]

Rhett explained how the United States was really operating as two countries already, and it only made sense to separate in peace. He said, "That identity of feelings, interests and institutions, which once existed, is gone. They are now divided between agricultural and manufacturing, and commercial states, between slaveholding, and non-slaveholding states. Their institutions and industrial pursuits have made them totally different peoples."[212] He furthered, "They desire to establish a sectional despotism, not only omnipotent in congress, but omnipotent over the states; and as if to manifest the imperious necessity of our secession, they threaten with the sword, to coerce submission to their rule."[213]

Rhett closed his appeal for southern nation building thusly:

> *All we demand of other peoples is, to be let alone, to work out our own high destinies. United together, and we must be the most independent, as we are among the most important, of the nations of the world. United together, and we require no other instrument to conquer peace, than our beneficent productions. United together, and we must be a great, free and prosperous people, whose renown must spread throughout the civilized world, and pass down, we trust, to the remotest ages. We ask you to join us, in forming a Confederacy of Slaveholding States.*[214]

At the same time, Charlestonian Christopher Memminger was charged with heading a committee to draft a document explaining the cause for secession. The final product was the *Declaration of the Immediate Causes Which Induce and Justify the Secession of South Carolina from the Federal Union.* Not as long and thorough as Rhett's *Address of the People of South Carolina, Assembled in Convention, to the People of the Slaveholding States of the United States*, the document stated that the main cause for the separation was "increasing hostility on part of the non-slaveholding states to the institution of slavery." The document charged the federal government with allowing organizations such as the Underground Railroad to operate; publications such as the *Liberator* and novels such as *Uncle Tom's Cabin*, which they claimed incited rebellion, to exist; and the formation of the Republican Party, which politicized slavery, to ascend to the executive office.

It is not surprising that South Carolina moved so swiftly for secession following the election of Abraham Lincoln since his platform offered nothing to the South. South Carolina governor Francis Wilkinson Pickens had been in contact with other southern governors but did not wait for the other cotton states to act. South Carolina took the lead.

The threat of secession had been thrown around so often by both North and South that it seemed a rather common way to solve differences. After generations of discussion and threats, South Carolina finally heeded the words of the Declaration of Independence: "[P]rudence, indeed, will dictate that governments long established should not be changed for light and transient causes." South Carolina fully believed that states' rights were critical and that the threat of secession was a legitimate tool for getting what a state or group of states wanted. So, when South Carolinians finally seceded from the Union in December 1860, they were fulfilling their forefathers' goals at the Second Continental Congress.

South Carolinians felt that by resisting the federal government, they were fulfilling the American Revolutionary ideals of resisting central authority to maintain local autonomy. How could the founding fathers or framers of the Constitution have ever forbidden the right of secession or ever dreamed of secession as illegitimate? After all, the United States Constitution did not address the withdrawal of a state from the compact, so South Carolinians interpreted their tenure in the United States and their adherence to the Constitution as a document to be held "at will." Like the founding fathers, who based "our Lives, our Fortunes and our sacred Honor" on the enlightened idea that people have the God-given right to shake off perceived tyranny and create new governments in order to safeguard their future, South Carolinians acted.

After years of preparation, the people of Georgetown and Horry united with the rest of the Lowcountry and finally convinced the upcountry to join them in an alliance to each other and for their independence from the United States on the grounds that their rights had been trampled and their calls for redress ignored.

Appendix I

1850 Agricultural Survey of All Saints Parish[215]

Agricultural Product	*Dr. John D. Magill*	*Dr. Andrew Hasell*	*William Algernon Allston*	*John H. Tucker*	*Lieutenant Governor Joshua John Ward*	*Plowden C.J. Weston*
improved acres	317	16	1,400	375	3,117	300
unimproved acres	3,000	375	--	--	7,000	400
cash value of farms	$40,000	$8,200	$200,000	$85,000	$527,000	$110,000
value of farming implements and machinery	$1,200	$100	$1,000	$500	$2,500	48,500
horses	26	3	15	11	51	--
asses and mules	6	5	5	4	49	16
milch cows	15	6	--	10	285	4
working oxen	15	--	--	25	200	40
other cattle	100	75	--	50	400	--
sheep	81	75	--	51	219	--

Agricultural Product	*Dr. John D. Magill*	*Dr. Andrew Hasell*	*William Algernon Allston*	*John H. Tucker*	*Lieutenant Governor Joshua John Ward*	*Plowden C.J. Weston*
swine	40	--	--	159	450	--
value of livestock	$2,862	$975	$1,000	$2,200	$34,808	$1,000
bushels of Indian corn	1,500	850	--	2,800	7,000	50
bushels of oats	300	--	--	60	2,000	40
pounds of rice	420,000	--	1,800,000	300,000	2,900,000	315,800
four-hundred-pound bales of ginned cotton	--	--	--	--	--	--
pounds of wool	160	150	--	100	600	1,625
bushels of peas and beans	--	--	--	--	1,000	1,000
bushels of irish potatoes	--	--	--	--	--	--
bushels of sweet potatoes	1,000	--	--	1,000	66,000	74,000
value of orchard products	--	--	--	--	--	--
pounds of butter	100	--	--	--	500	1,140

Appendix II

1850 Agricultural Survey of Prince George Winyah Parish[216]

Agricultural Product	*Rep. John Harrelson Read Jr.*	*Dr. James Ritchie Sparkman*	*Senator Robert F.W. Allston*	*Reverend Maurice Harvey Lance**	*Joel Roberts Poinsett*	*Dr. Edward Thomas Heriot*	*Dr. Francis S. Parker*
improved acres	100	200	1,350	640	270	249	370
unimproved acres	500	4,300	4,200	1,400	400	1,549	1,500
cash value of farm	$20,000	$28,000	$120,000	$54,000	$30,000	$37,000	$25,000
value of farming implements and machinery	$150	$400	$5,000	$800	$300	$500	$400
horses	1	7	18	5	4	5	4
asses and mules	2	6	6	9	3	6	5
milch cows	--	6	40	10	15	6	10
working oxen	--	10	45	12	8	8	12
other cattle	--	14	80	44	--	20	8
sheep	--	50	100	62	--	47	20

Agricultural Product	*Rep. John Harrelson Read Jr.*	*Dr. James Ritchie Sparkman*	*Senator Robert F.W. Allston*	*Reverend Maurice Harvey Lance**	*Joel Roberts Poinsett*	*Dr. Edward Thomas Heriot*	*Dr. Francis S. Parker*
swine	--	--	100	--	--	--	--
value of livestock	$150	$1,692	$5,230	$1,420	$690	$1,026	$890
bushels of rye	--	10	100	--	--	15	--
bushels of Indian corn	500	800	16,000	2,400	400	150	800
bushels of oats	--	140	400	500	200	100	500
pounds of rice	150,000	196,000	840,000	670,000	200,000	300,000	375,000
pounds of wool	--	100	250	136	--	60	50
bushels of peas and beans	62	--	400	--	--	--	300
bushels of sweet potatoes	--	18,060	6,000	1,200	1,000	--	300
pounds of butter	--	20	150	--	100	--	--
tons of hay	--	--	--	--	--	--	--
bushels of grass seed	--	--	--	--	--	--	--
pounds of honey	--	--	--	--	--	--	--

Appendix III

1860 Agricultural Survey of All Saints Parish[217]

Agricultural Product	*Dr. John D. Magill*	*Dr. Andrew Hasell*	*Daniel W. Jordan*	*Estate of John H. Tucker*	*Estate of Lieutenant Governor Joshua John Ward*	*Lieutenant Governor Plowden C.J. Weston*
improved acres	635	180	900	2,600	5,500	900
unimproved acres	2,265	300	1,300	10,000	10,100	2,171
cash value of farms	$70,000	$2,000	$125,000	$300,000	$380,000	$142,000
value of farming implements and machinery	$2,000	$100	$27,000	$30,000	$75,000	$3,000
horses	15	4	9	--	29	7
asses and mules	7	2	51	7	39	13
milch cows	20	2	15	20	102	89
working oxen	12	--	38	16	170	54
other cattle	100	2	110	45	420	16
sheep	109	--	27	16	171	44
swine	56	15	100	75	447	300

Agricultural Product	*Dr. John D. Magill*	*Dr. Andrew Hasell*	*Daniel W. Jordan*	*Estate of John H. Tucker*	*Estate of Lieutenant Governor Joshua John Ward*	*Lieutenant Governor Plowden C.J. Weston*
value of livestock	$6,760	$900	$6,934	$2,755	$16,350	$6,558
bushels of Indian corn	2,000	300	--	4,360	10,250	200
bushels of oats	300	--	--	--	500	--
pounds of rice	450,000	--	--	1,530,000	4,410,000	1,252,000
four-hundred-pound bales of ginned cotton	--	--	8	--	--	--
pounds of wool	300	--	--	--	342	--
bushels of peas and beans	400	75	1,900	500	--	50
bushels of Irish potatoes	--	--	7	--	--	--
bushels of sweet potatoes	3,000	800	1,200	8,000	--	100
value of orchard products	$20	--	--	--	--	--
pounds of butter	100	--	50	--	--	25
tons of hay	--	--	100	--	--	--
pounds of beeswax	5	--	--	--	--	50
pounds of honey	40	--	--	--	--	--
value of homemade manufacturing	--	--	$35,000	--	--	--
value of animals slaughtered	$400	$75	$2,190	--	--	$100

Appendix IV

1860 Agricultural Survey of Prince George Winyah Parish[218]

Agricultural Product	*Rep. John Harrelson Read Jr.*	*Dr. James Ritchie Sparkman*	*Governor Robert F.W. Allston*	*Reverend Maurice Harvey Lance*	*Dr. Francis S. Parker*	*Georgetown District*	*South Carolina*
improved acres	1,350	400	2,000	450	429	50,858	4,573,000
unimproved acres	--	2,300	4,450	1,000	2,250	309,083	11,023,850
cash value of farm	$185,000	$65,000	$100,000	30,000	$100,000	$5,818,000	$130,652,508
value of farming implements and machinery	$30,000	$2,000	$12,000	$500	$10,000	$616,774	$6,151,657
horses	10	5	15	4	6	811	81,125
asses and mules	15	5	11	8	15	661	56,456
milch cows	20	17	30	6	10	2,376	163,938
working oxen	30	12	55	8	8	1,450	23,020
other cattle	90	25	100	25	4	6,611	320,209

Agricultural Product	*Rep. John Harrelson Read Jr.*	*Dr. James Ritchie Sparkman*	*Governor Robert F.W. Allston*	*Reverend Maurice Harvey Lance*	*Dr. Francis S. Parker*	*Georgetown District*	*South Carolina*
sheep	140	46	200	50	50	4,666	233,500
swine	--	125	--	--	--	11,416	965,779
value of livestock	$3,800	$1,800	$6,000	$1,500	$3,150	$310,710	$23,931,405
bushels of rye	--	20	100	--	--	460	89,091
bushels of Indian corn	8,600	700	3,000	1,500	3,000	339,373	15,065,606
bushels of oats	2,100	--	800	250	--	8,755	936,974
pounds of rice	1,575,000	400,000	1,500,000	560,000	1,440,000	55,805,385	119,100,528
pounds of wool	280	75	560	100	--	7,054	427,102
bushels of peas and beans	500	300	1,000	--	30	19,270	1,728,674
bushels of sweet potatoes	1,000	3,000	12,000	--	2,000	139,970	4,115,688
pounds of butter	200	100	500	--	--	16,030	3,177,934
tons of hay	--	--	6	--	--	745	87,587
bushels of grass seed	--	--	8	--	--	8	38
pounds of honey	--	--	80	--	--	3,199	526,077
value of animals slaughtered	$500	[illegible]	$1,000	--	--	$38,710	$6,072,822

Appendix V

Representatives in the General Assembly

Year/ District	*All Saints Parish (includes Horry and Georgetown Districts east of the Waccamaw River)*	*Kingston Parish (Horry District)*	*Prince George Winyah Parish (Georgetown District)*
1832	Joshua John Ward	John W. Pickett	Anthony White Dozier, Peter William Fraser and Solomon Cohen Jr.
1833	Joshua John Ward	John W. Pickett	Anthony White Dozier, Peter William Fraser and Solomon Cohen Jr.
1834	Joshua John Ward	John W. Pickett	Allard Henry Belin, John William Coachman and Solomon Cohen Jr.
1835	Joshua John Ward	John W. Pickett	Allard Henry Belin, John William Coachman and Solomon Cohen Jr.
1836	Joseph Alston	John Wesley Durant	Allard Henry Belin, Thomas G. Carr and John William Coachman
1837	Joseph Alston	John Wesley Durant	Allard Henry Belin, Thomas G. Carr and John William Coachman

Year/ District	*All Saints Parish (includes Horry and Georgetown Districts east of the Waccamaw River)*	*Kingston Parish (Horry District)*	*Prince George Winyah Parish (Georgetown District)*
1838	Joseph Alston	James Beatty	Allard Henry Belin, Thomas G. Carr and John Izard Middleton
1839	Joseph Alston	James Beatty	Allard Henry Belin, Thomas G. Carr and John Izard Middleton
1840	Thomas S. Randall	James Beatty	Allard Henry Belin, Thomas G. Carr and John Izard Middleton
1841	Thomas S. Randall	James Beatty	Allard Henry Belin, Thomas G. Carr and John Izard Middleton
1842	John Ashe Alston	Garret Gowan	Allard Henry Belin, Thomas G. Carr and John Izard Middleton
1843	John Ashe Alston	Garret Gowan	Allard Henry Belin, James Ritchie Sparkman and John Izard Middleton
1844	John Ashe Alston	Garret Gowan	Peter William Fraser, John Izard Middleton and John Harleston Read Jr.
1845	John Ashe Alston	Garret Gowan (died 1845) and Arthur H. Crawford (qualified November 24, 1845)	Peter William Fraser, John Izard Middleton and John Harleston Read Jr.
1846	John Ashe Alston	Charles Murrell	Samuel Taylor Atkinson, John Izard Middleton and John Harleston Read Jr.
1847	John Ashe Alston	Charles Murrell	Gabriel Manigault, John Izard Middleton and John Harleston Read Jr.
1848	John Ashe Alston	Rueben George Weston Grissette	John B. Easterling, John Izard Middleton (became Speaker of the House) and John Harleston Read Jr.
1849	John Ashe Alston	Rueben George Weston Grissette	John B. Easterling, John Izard Middleton and John Harleston Read Jr.

Year/ District	*All Saints Parish (includes Horry and Georgetown Districts east of the Waccamaw River)*	*Kingston Parish (Horry District)*	*Prince George Winyah Parish (Georgetown District)*
1850	Daniel William Jordan	Rueben George Weston Grissette	Gabriel Manigault, John Izard Middleton and John Harleston Read Jr.
1851	Daniel William Jordan	Rueben George Weston Grissette	Gabriel Manigault, John Izard Middleton and John Harleston Read Jr.
1852	Allard Belin Flagg	Robert Munro Jr.	Gabriel Manigault, John Izard Middleton and John Harleston Read Jr.
1853	Allard Belin Flagg	Robert Munro Jr.	Gabriel Manigault, John Izard Middleton and John Harleston Read Jr.
1854	Thomas S. Randall	Robert Munro Jr.	John Izard Middleton, John Harleston Read Jr. and Benjamin Henry Wilson
1855	Thomas S. Randall	Robert Munro Jr.	John Izard Middleton, John Harleston Read Jr. and Benjamin Henry Wilson
1856	Plowden Charles Jennett Weston	William I. Graham	John Izard Middleton (resigned to fill Robert F.W. Allston's seat in the Senate when he became governor), Richard Dozier, John Harleston Read Jr. and Benjamin Henry Wilson
1857	Plowden Charles Jennett Weston	William I. Graham	Richard Dozier, John Harleston Read Jr. and Benjamin Henry Wilson
1858	Peter Vaught Sr.	Joseph F. Harrell	Richard Dozier, John Harleston Read Jr. and John Hyrne Tucker Jr.
1859	Peter Vaught Sr.	Joseph F. Harell	Richard Dozier, John Harleston Read Jr. and John Hyrne Tucker Jr.
1860	Peter Vaught Sr.	Cornelius Benjamin Sarvis	Richard Dozier, John Harleston Read Jr. and Plowden Charles Jennett Weston

Year/ District	*All Saints Parish (includes Horry and Georgetown Districts east of the Waccamaw River)*	*Kingston Parish (Horry District)*	*Prince George Winyah Parish (Georgetown District)*
1861	Peter Vaught Sr.	Cornelius Benjamin Sarvis	Richard Dozier, John Harleston Read Jr. and Plowden Charles Jennett Weston (Weston was elected lieutenant governor in 1862)

Appendix VI

South Carolina State Senators

Year	*All Saints Parish (includes Horry and Georgetown District east of the Waccamaw River)*	*Kingston Parish (Horry District)*	*Prince George Winyah Parish (Georgetown District)*
1832	Joseph Waites Allston	Benjamin Gause	Robert F.W. Allston
1833	Thomas Pinckney Alston	Benjamin Gause	Robert F.W. Allston
1834	Thomas Pinckney Alston	Henry Durant	Robert F.W. Allston
1835	Thomas Pinckney Alston	Henry Durant	Robert F.W. Allston
1836	Thomas Pinckney Alston	Henry Durant	Robert F.W. Allston
1837	Thomas Pinckney Alston	Henry Durant (died June 6, 1837) and Robert Munro (qualified November 27, 1837)	Robert F.W. Allston
1838	Edward Thomas Heriot	Robert Munro	Robert F.W. Allston
1839	Edward Thomas Heriot	Robert Munro	Robert F.W. Allston
1840	Edward Thomas Heriot	William H. Johnston	Robert F.W. Allston
1841	Edward Thomas Heriot	William H. Johnston	Robert F.W. Allston
1842	Joshua John Ward	Josias Tillman Sessions	Robert F.W. Allston
1843	Joshua John Ward	Josias Tillman Session (resigned to become sheriff of Horry District) and Joel B. Skipper (qualified November 27, 1843)	Robert F.W. Allston

Year	*All Saints Parish (includes Horry and Georgetown District east of the Waccamaw River)*	*Kingston Parish (Horry District)*	*Prince George Winyah Parish (Georgetown District)*
1844	Joshua John Ward	Joel B. Skipper	Robert F.W. Allston
1845	Joshua John Ward	Joel B. Skipper	Robert F.W. Allston
1846	Joshua John Ward	Joel B. Skipper	Robert F.W. Allston
1847	Joshua John Ward	Joel B. Skipper	Robert F.W. Allston
1848	Joshua John Ward	Joel B. Skipper	Robert F.W. Allston
1849	Joshua John Ward	Joel B. Skipper	Robert F.W. Allston
1850	Joshua John Ward (elected lieutenant governor; resigned seat)	Joel B. Skipper	Robert F.W. Allston (served as president of the Senate)
1851	Andrew Hasell	Joel B. Skipper	Robert F.W. Allston (served as president of the Senate)
1852	Andrew Hasell	Rueben George Weston Grissette	Robert F.W. Allston (served as president of the Senate)
1853	Andrew Hasell	Rueben George Weston Grissette	Robert F.W. Allston (served as president of the Senate)
1854	Andrew Hasell	Rueben George Weston Grissette	Robert F.W. Allston (served as president of the Senate)
1855	Andrew Hasell	Rueben George Weston Grissette	Robert F.W. Allston (served as president of the Senate)
1856	Andrew Hasell	James Beatty	Robert F.W. Allston (elected governor; resigned seat)
1857	Andrew Hasell	James Beatty	John Izard Middleton
1858	Charles Alston	Francis Ichabod Sessions	Benjamin H. Wilson
1859	Charles Alston	Francis Ichabod Sessions	Benjamin H. Wilson
1860	Charles Alston	Francis Ichabod Sessions	Benjamin H. Wilson
1861	James J. Wortham	Francis Ichabod Sessions	Benjamin H. Wilson

Notes

Introduction

1. Lathers and Sanborn, *Reminiscences of Richard Lathers*, 5.
2. Boney, *Southerners All*, 13.
3. Childs, *Rice Planter and Sportsman*, 6.
4. United States Bureau of Census, *Agricultural Survey of Horry District*, 1850.
5. Ibid., *South Carolina Industry Schedule*, 1850; *South Carolina Industry Schedule*, 1860.
6. Interview with Robert McAlister, Georgetown Maritime Museum, August 10, 2016.
7. Boney, *Southerners All*, 41–42.
8. Ibid., 61.
9. Ibid., 59.
10. Ibid., 62.
11. DeBow, "Interest in Slavery," 169–77.
12. Ibid., 171.
13. United States Bureau of Census, *Agricultural Survey of Horry District*, 1860.

Chapter 2

14. Allston, *Eulogy on John C. Calhoun*, 11.
15. Rogers, *History of Georgetown County*, 234.
16. Silverman, "South Carolina," 2.

17. Allston, *Eulogy on John C. Calhoun*, 12.
18. Kennig, *Great South Carolinians*, 303–4.
19. Ibid., 312–13.
20. Childs, *Rice Planter and Sportsman*, 25.
21. *Winyah Intelligencer*, "States' Rights Convention in Charleston," February 8, 1832; Allard H. Belin, John A. Keith, Dr. Aaron Lopez and J. Walter Phillips attended the meeting with Alston.
22. Rogers, *History of Georgetown County*, 239.
23. Boucher, *Nullification Controversy in South Carolina*, 231.
24. Rogers, *History of Georgetown County*, 245.
25. Devereux, *Life and Times of Robert F.W. Allston*, 72–73.
26. Boucher, *Nullification Controversy in South Carolina*, 307.
27. Rogers, *History of Georgetown County*, 246.
28. Ibid., 239–40.
29. Devereux, *Life and Times of Robert F.W. Allston*, 73.
30. *Winyah Intelligencer*, January 2, 1833.
31. Rogers, *History of Georgetown County*, 239.
32. *Winyah Observer*, "Profanity—Don't Do It," March 3, 1847; "Depend Upon Yourself and God Will Lead You," December 14, 1850.
33. *Winyah Observer*, "Book of Mormon," July 14, 1841.
34. *Pee Dee Times*, "Illustration of Mormonism," February 2, 1857.
35. *Winyah Observer*, "Anti-Sabbath Convention," March 3, 1848.
36. Boney, *Southerners All*, 25–26.
37. Lathers and Sanborn, *Reminiscences of Richard Lathers*, 6.
38. *Winyah Observer*, "Good Wife," April 7, 1841.
39. Ibid., "Woman: Her Mission and Destiny," November 11, 1844; "Diffusion of Christianity," November 18, 1844; "Worth of a Woman," November 20, 1844, and May 23, 1852.
40. Ibid., "Domestic Training" and "Women," November 1, 1848.
41. *Pee Dee Times*, "Wife's Devotion; or the Chivalry of Love," April 18, 1855; "Recipe for Getting a Husband," July 11, 1855; "Devotion of a True Woman," September 19, 1855; "Marrying Advice to Ladies," October 7, 1857.
42. *Winyah Observer*, "How to Treat a Wife," July 9, 1851.
43. Ibid., May 8, 1841.
44. *Georgetown American*, "Drinking, Vending and Making Ardent Spirits," November 30, 1839; *Winyah Observer*, "Temperance Oath," February 26, 1842; "Washingtonian's Temperance Oath," July 23, 1842.
45. *Pee Dee Times*, "Fanaticism," June 7, 1854.
46. Jones, *Plantation South*, 178–79.

Chapter 3

47. Devereux, *Life and Times of Robert F.W. Allston*, 76 and 81.
48. *Georgetown American*, "Second Declaration of Independence," August 5, 1840.
49. *Winyah Observer*, July 7, 1842.
50. Ibid., "Welfare of Our Town," April 10, 1841.
51. Ibid., May 8, 1841; July 6, 1844.
52. Rogers, *History of Georgetown County*, 208.
53. *Georgetown American*, "Battalion Order," July 3, 1840; "Battalion Orders," July 10, 1840; "Battalion Orders," August 12, 1840; "Battalion Orders," September 2, 1840.
54. Lathers and Sanborn, *Reminiscences of Richard Lathers*, 10.
55. *Georgetown American*, "Celebration of the Anniversary of Washington's Birth," February 17, 1841.
56. Lathers and Sanborn, *Reminiscences of Richard Lathers*, 18.
57. *Winyah Observer*, "Military Parade at Black Mingo," December 6, 1843; "Celebration of the 22," February 24, 1844.
58. Ibid., "Proceedings of the Democratic State Rights Party," June 9, 1841.
59. Lathers and Sanborn, *Reminiscences of Richard Lathers*, 35.
60. *Winyah Observer*, "Martin Van Buren," May 4, 1844.
61. Ibid., "Annexation," May 4, 1844.
62. Ibid., May 4, 1844.
63. Ibid., "Celebration of the 4th on the Pee Dee," July 13, 1844.
64. Silverman, "South Carolina," 2.
65. *Winyah Observer*, "Annexation of Canada," February 8, 1845.
66. Ibid., "State of the Poll," September 9, 1845.
67. Ibid., "Horry Celebration," July 4, 1845.
68. Ibid.
69. Ibid.
70. Ibid., "Anniversary of Our National Independence," July 12, 1845.
71. Ibid., "Repeal of the Corn Laws," March 11, 1846.
72. Scrolled across the masthead, *Winyah Observer*, December 8, 1847.
73. *Winyah Observer*, "Escape of the Paredes," September 1, 1847; "From New Mexico and the Plains," April 19, 1848.
74. Lathers and Sanborn, *Reminiscences of Richard Lathers*, 12.
75. *Winyah Observer*, "Day at Lowell," November 11, 1846.
76. Ibid., "Head Quarters 8th Regiment Cavalry, Order No. 8," May 3, 1848.

77. Ibid., "Australian Cotton," December 8, 1847.
78. Ibid., "Democratic Party Meeting," April 12, 1848; "Whig Party Meeting," May 17, 1848.
79. Ibid., "North and South: Van Buren, Cass and Taylor: Which Can the South Support?," August, 9, 1848.
80. Silverman, "South Carolina," 3.
81. *Winyah Observer*, February 7, 1849.
82. Ibid., April 18, 1849.
83. Ibid., "On Annexation of Canada," July 18, 1849.
84. Ibid., "District Meeting," April 11, 1849.
85. Ibid.
86. *Charleston Courier*, "Meeting at Conwayboro," April 21, 1849.
87. *Winyah Observer*, "4th of July at Johnsonville," July 18, 1849.
88. Ibid., "Fourth of July Celebration," July 4, 1849.
89. Ibid., "Who Has Betrayed the South?" July 25, 1849.
90. *Washington Union*, "Southern State Convention," October 17, 1849.
91. *Winyah Observer*, "Railroad Convention in Memphis," May 12, 1852.
92. Ibid., "Slavery Question," January 19, 1850.
93. Ibid., "In Congress," February 2, 1850.
94. Ibid., "Mr. Calhoun's Speech," March 9, 1850; "Mr. Calhoun's Speech," March 16, 1850.
95. *True Republican*, "Southern Convention," February 13, 1850.
96. *Winyah Observer*, "Head Quarters 8th Brigade, S.C.M" and "Head Quarters of Lower Battalion," February 27, 1850.
97. Ibid., "Mr. Calhoun's Death," April 3, 1850.
98. Allston, *Eulogy on John C. Calhoun*, 3.
99. Ibid., 8.
100. Ibid., 16–17.
101. Ibid., 20.
102. Lathers and Sanborn, *Reminiscences of Richard Lathers*, 27.
103. Devereux, *Life and Times of Robert F.W. Allston*, 149.
104. Easterby, *South Carolina Rice Plantation*, 102.
105. Ibid., 99.
106. *Charleston Courier*, "4th of July Celebration at Conwayboro," July 16, 1850.
107. *Winyah Observer*, "Slavery and the Constitution," May 1, 1850.
108. Ibid., "Southern Convention at Nashville," June 19, 1850; "Slavery Question and the Missouri Compromise," August 7, 1850; "Battle of King's Mountain; or Hero's Revenge," October 9, 1850.

109. Ibid., "Georgetown and All Saints Southern Rights Association," October 16, 1850; "Georgetown and All Saints Southern Rights Association," October 23, 1850.
110. Ibid., November 13, 1850, and November 18, 1850.
111. Ibid., "Divisions of the South," November 18, 1850.

Chapter 4

112. Reynolds and Faunt, *Biographical Directory of the Senate of South Carolina*, 44–58.
113. Ibid.; Rogers, *History of Georgetown County*, 327, 242 and 250.
114. *Winyah Observer*, "Southern Rights Association of All Saints Parish," December 11, 1850.
115. Ibid., "Policy of the South," February 12, 1851.
116. Ibid., "Story of the Cowpens," April 12, 1851; "First Secession of South Carolina," June 11, 1851.
117. Ibid., "Convention of Southern Rights Association," May 14, 1851.
118. Ibid., "4th of July," July 7, 1851; the *Winyah Observer* on June 23, 1851, announced John Harleston Read Jr.'s reelection to lead the militia.
119. *Winyah Observer*, September 9, 1851.
120. Ibid., "Right of Secession," October 8, 1851.
121. Ibid., "Great Secession Demonstration: Mass-Meeting at Morris Ferry 700 Persons Present," October 15, 1851.
122. Ibid.
123. Ibid., "Character of Marion," November 15, 1851; "Patrick Henry," May 19, 1852; "Battle of New Orleans," October 13, 1852.
124. Ibid., "What Constitutes Citizenship?" January 28, 1852.
125. Ibid., "Age of Can't," August 18, 1852.
126. Reynolds and Faunt, *Biographical Directory of the Senate of South Carolina*, 172; Silverman, "South Carolina," 4; *Winyah Observer*, May 5, 1852.
127. Rogers, *History of Georgetown County*, 362.
128. *Winyah Observer*, December 1, 1852, and December 15, 1852.
129. *Pee Dee Times*, "What Makes South Carolina So Great," March 9, 1853. Waterman's last edition was published on April, 19, 1854.
130. Ibid. *Times*, "New York Conventions," August 10, 1853; "Is an Abolitionist a Gentleman," April 6, 1853; "Charity and Philanthropy," April 20, 1853; "Fanaticism," June 7, 1854; "More Abolitionist Outrages," September 20, 1854.

131. Ibid., "Harriet Beecher Stowe's Charity," May 11, 1853.
132. Ibid., "Condition of the Colored Population of the North," July 20, 1853.
133. Ibid., "Slavery—the Proper Condition of the Negro," August 2, 1854.
134. Childs, *Rice Planter and Sportsman*, 49.
135. James Henry Hammond, "Mud-Sill Speech," in *Slavery Defended*, 123.
136. *Pee Dee Times*, "Negro Freedom and Slavery," February 22, 1854.
137. Ibid., "Northern Negro Life," September 13, 1854.
138. Ibid., "Rising Storm," January 25, 1854.
139. Ibid., "Fourth of July on Pee Dee," July 9, 1854.
140. Ibid., "More of the Fourth," July 12, 1854.
141. Ibid., "Who Were the Slave Traders," November 22, 1854, and November 29, 1854.
142. Ibid., "Abolition of Negro Slavery," September 3, 1856.
143. Ibid., "New Schemes of Disunion," March 14, 1855.
144. Ibid., "Rising Trouble in Kansas," May 30, 1855.
145. Ibid., "Kansas," December 12, 1855.
146. Ibid., "How Changed," August 29, 1855.
147. Ibid., "Political Excitement," August 29, 1855.
148. Ibid., "Trade with the North," September 5, 1855.
149. Ibid., "Military Capacity of the South," August 22, 1855.
150. Ibid., "To Kansas Emigrants and to All Friends of the South," February 6, 1856.
151. Ibid., "Kansas Meeting in All Saints," March 5, 1856.
152. Ibid., "Kansas Meeting," March 12, 1856; "Kansas," March 21, 1856, and March 26, 1856.
153. Ibid., "Kansas Meeting," March 12, 1856.
154. Easterby, *South Carolina Rice Plantation*, 131.
155. Ibid., 130–31.
156. *Pee Dee Times*, "Kansas," April, 30, 1856.
157. Ibid., May 14, 1856.

Chapter 5

158. Silverman, "South Carolina," 5.
159. *Pee Dee Times*, July 9, 1856.
160. Ibid., "Brooks Dinner," October 15, 1856.
161. Silverman, "South Carolina," 7.

162. *Pee Dee Times*, "Sign of the Times," August 6, 1856; "Form a Southern Confederacy," November 5, 1856.
163. Ibid., "What Constitutes a Gentleman," May 14, 1856.
164. Silverman, "South Carolina," 5.
165. *Pee Dee Times*, "Mr. Buchanan in Favor," August 20, 1856.
166. *Winyah Observer*, "Gallery of Industry and Enterprise," May 12, 1852.
167. Pringle, *Chronicles of Chicora Wood*, 20; *Winyah Observer*, October 2, 1850; May 12, 1852; *Pee Dee Times*, March 12, 1856.
168. Reynolds and Faunt, *Biographical Directory of the Senate of South Carolina*, 171–72.
169. Easterby, *South Carolina Rice Plantation*, 132.
170. Weston, *Documents Connected with the History of South Carolina*, 3–4. In the editor's note, Weston claimed that he compiled the documents from English collections in an attempt to help stimulate research by the South Carolina Historical Society.
171. Phillips, *Plantation and Frontier Documents*, vol. 1, 115–22.
172. Weston, *Address by Plowden C.J. Weston*, 7.
173. Rogers, *History of Georgetown County*.
174. Carolana, www.carolana.com.
175. *Pee Dee Times*, "Death and Funeral of Mr. Brooks of South Carolina," February 4, 1857.
176. Ibid., "Decision of the Supreme Court Case," March 18, 1857.
177. Ibid., "Headquarters," March 4, 1857.
178. Ibid., "Governors Review," March 25, 1857.
179. Ibid., "Duty of Southern Men," June 10, 1857.
180. Ibid., "Sign of the Times," May 6, 1857.
181. Weston, *Address by Plowden C.J. Weston*, 3.
182. Ibid., 4.
183. Ibid., 6–7.
184. Ibid., 7–8.
185. Ibid., 7.
186. Ibid., 9.
187. Ibid., 12–13.
188. Ibid., 9.
189. Ibid., 15–16.
190. Allston, *Message No. 1, of His Excellency R.F.W. Allston*, 3.
191. Ibid., 11–12.
192. Ibid., 14.
193. Ibid.

194. *Pee Dee Times*, "Address Delivered by Plowden C.J. Weston," August 5, 1857; "Message No. 1. of His Excellency R.F.W. Allston," December 2, 1857.
195. Ibid., "Message No. 1. of His Excellency R.F.W. Allston," August 21, 1857; Allston, *Message No. 1, of His Excellency R.F.W. Allston*, 16.
196. *Pee Dee Times*, "Life in Northern Cities," July 22, 1857; "White Slavery in Massachusetts" and "Kansas Bleeds No More," September 30, 1857.

Chapter 6

197. *Selections from Letters and Speeches*, 317.
198. Hammond, "Mud-Sill Speech," *Slavery Defended*, 121–22.
199. *Pee Dee Times*, "Southern Commercial Convention in Montgomery," April 21, 1858.
200. Ibid., "4th of July," May 12, 1858.
201. Ibid., July 7, 1858.
202. Ibid.
203. Silverman, "South Carolina," 6.
204. Childs, *Rice Planter and Sportsman*, 130.
205. *Charleston Mercury*, November 8, 1860.
206. Lesser, *Relic of the Lost Cause*, 21–26.
207. *South Carolina Historical Magazine*, "Delegates to the South Carolina Secession Convention," 192–97.
208. Easterby, *South Carolina Rice Plantation*, 169–70.
209. Rogers, *History of Georgetown County*, 382.
210. Rhett, "Address of the People of South Carolina," 4–5.
211. Ibid., 6.
212. Ibid., 12.
213. Ibid., 14.
214. Ibid., 16.

Appendix I

215. South Carolina Department of Archives and History, *Agricultural Survey*, 1850.

Appendix II

216. Ibid. *Represents Reverend Lance and Mrs. Anna Maria Taylor Lance. They were separated at the time of the census, but all family assets are combined for this report.

Appendix III

217. South Carolina Department of Archives and History, *Agricultural Survey*, 1860.

Appendix IV

218. Ibid.

Bibliography

Allston, Robert F.W. *Eulogy on John C. Calhoun Pronounced at the Request of the Citizens of Georgetown District.* Charleston, SC: Miller and Brown, April 23, 1850.

———. *Message No. 1, of His Excellency R.F.W. Allston, Governor of South Carolina to the State and House of Representatives at the Session of 1857.* Columbia, SC: R.W. Gibbes State Printer, 1857.

Boney, F.N. *Southerners All.* Macon, GA: Mercer University Press, 1984.

Boucher, Chauncey Samuel. *The Nullification Controversy in South Carolina.* New York: Greenwood Press, 1968.

Burroughs, J. Benjamin. Interview with Robert McAlister, August 10, 2016.

Charleston Courier. "4th of July Celebration at Conwayboro." July 16, 1850.

———. "Meeting at Conwayboro." April 21, 1849.

———. November 8, 1860.

Childs, Arney B. *Rice Planter and Sportsman: The Recollections of J. Motte Alston, 1821–1909.* Columbia: University of South Carolina Press, 1953.

DeBow, J.D.B. "The Interest in Slavery of the Southern Non-Slaveholder." In *Slavery Defended: The Views of the Old South.* Englewood Cliffs, NJ: Prentice-Hall, 1963.

Devereux, Anthony Q. *The Life and Times of Robert F.W. Allston.* Columbia, SC: R.L. Bryan Company, 1976.

Easterby, J.H., ed. *The South Carolina Rice Plantation as Revealed in the Papers of Robert F.W. Allston.* Chicago: University of Chicago Press, 1945.

Georgetown American. "Battalion Order." July 3, 1840.

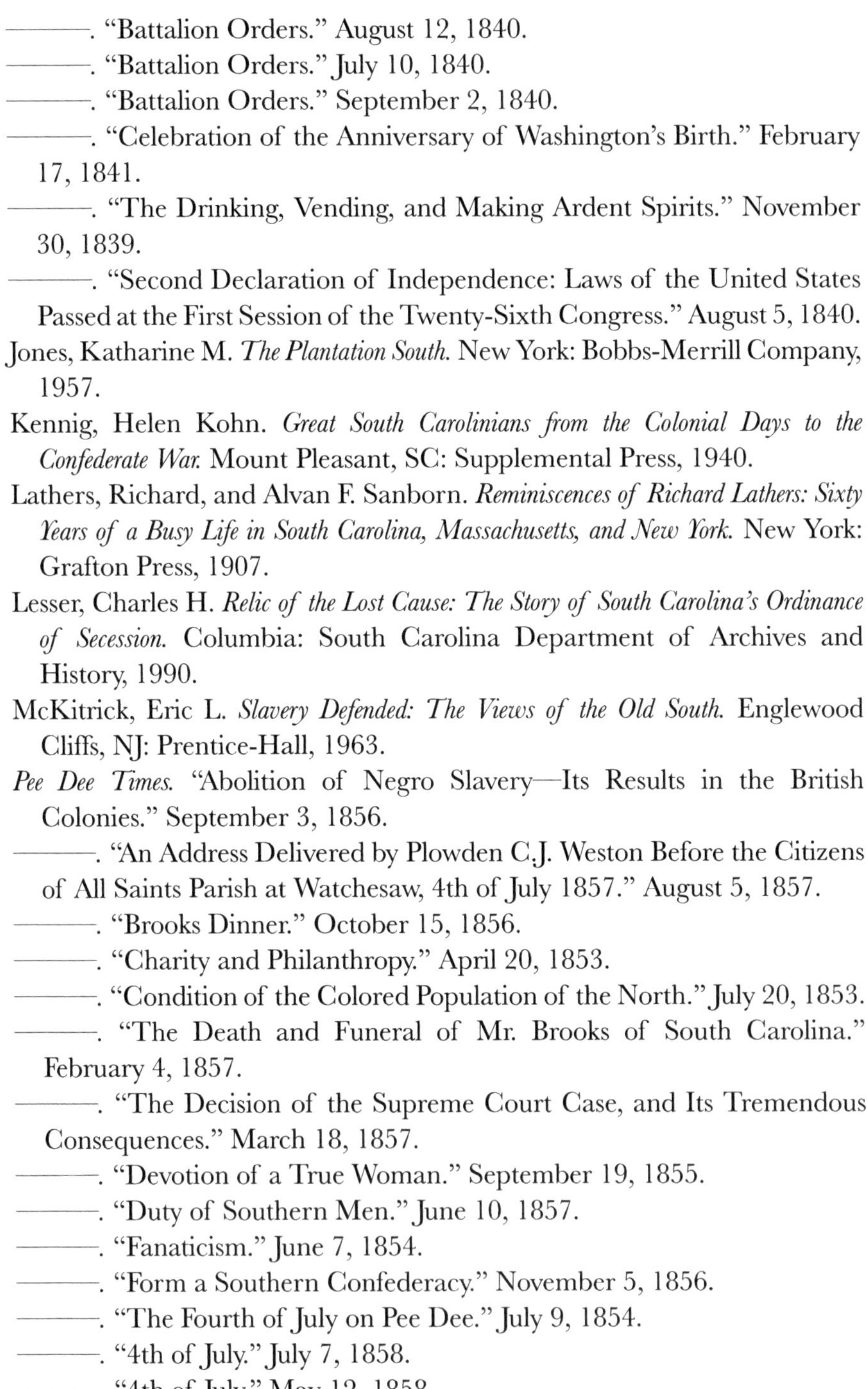

———. "Battalion Orders." August 12, 1840.

———. "Battalion Orders." July 10, 1840.

———. "Battalion Orders." September 2, 1840.

———. "Celebration of the Anniversary of Washington's Birth." February 17, 1841.

———. "The Drinking, Vending, and Making Ardent Spirits." November 30, 1839.

———. "Second Declaration of Independence: Laws of the United States Passed at the First Session of the Twenty-Sixth Congress." August 5, 1840.

Jones, Katharine M. *The Plantation South.* New York: Bobbs-Merrill Company, 1957.

Kennig, Helen Kohn. *Great South Carolinians from the Colonial Days to the Confederate War.* Mount Pleasant, SC: Supplemental Press, 1940.

Lathers, Richard, and Alvan F. Sanborn. *Reminiscences of Richard Lathers: Sixty Years of a Busy Life in South Carolina, Massachusetts, and New York.* New York: Grafton Press, 1907.

Lesser, Charles H. *Relic of the Lost Cause: The Story of South Carolina's Ordinance of Secession.* Columbia: South Carolina Department of Archives and History, 1990.

McKitrick, Eric L. *Slavery Defended: The Views of the Old South.* Englewood Cliffs, NJ: Prentice-Hall, 1963.

Pee Dee Times. "Abolition of Negro Slavery—Its Results in the British Colonies." September 3, 1856.

———. "An Address Delivered by Plowden C.J. Weston Before the Citizens of All Saints Parish at Watchesaw, 4th of July 1857." August 5, 1857.

———. "Brooks Dinner." October 15, 1856.

———. "Charity and Philanthropy." April 20, 1853.

———. "Condition of the Colored Population of the North." July 20, 1853.

———. "The Death and Funeral of Mr. Brooks of South Carolina." February 4, 1857.

———. "The Decision of the Supreme Court Case, and Its Tremendous Consequences." March 18, 1857.

———. "Devotion of a True Woman." September 19, 1855.

———. "Duty of Southern Men." June 10, 1857.

———. "Fanaticism." June 7, 1854.

———. "Form a Southern Confederacy." November 5, 1856.

———. "The Fourth of July on Pee Dee." July 9, 1854.

———. "4th of July." July 7, 1858.

———. "4th of July." May 12, 1858.

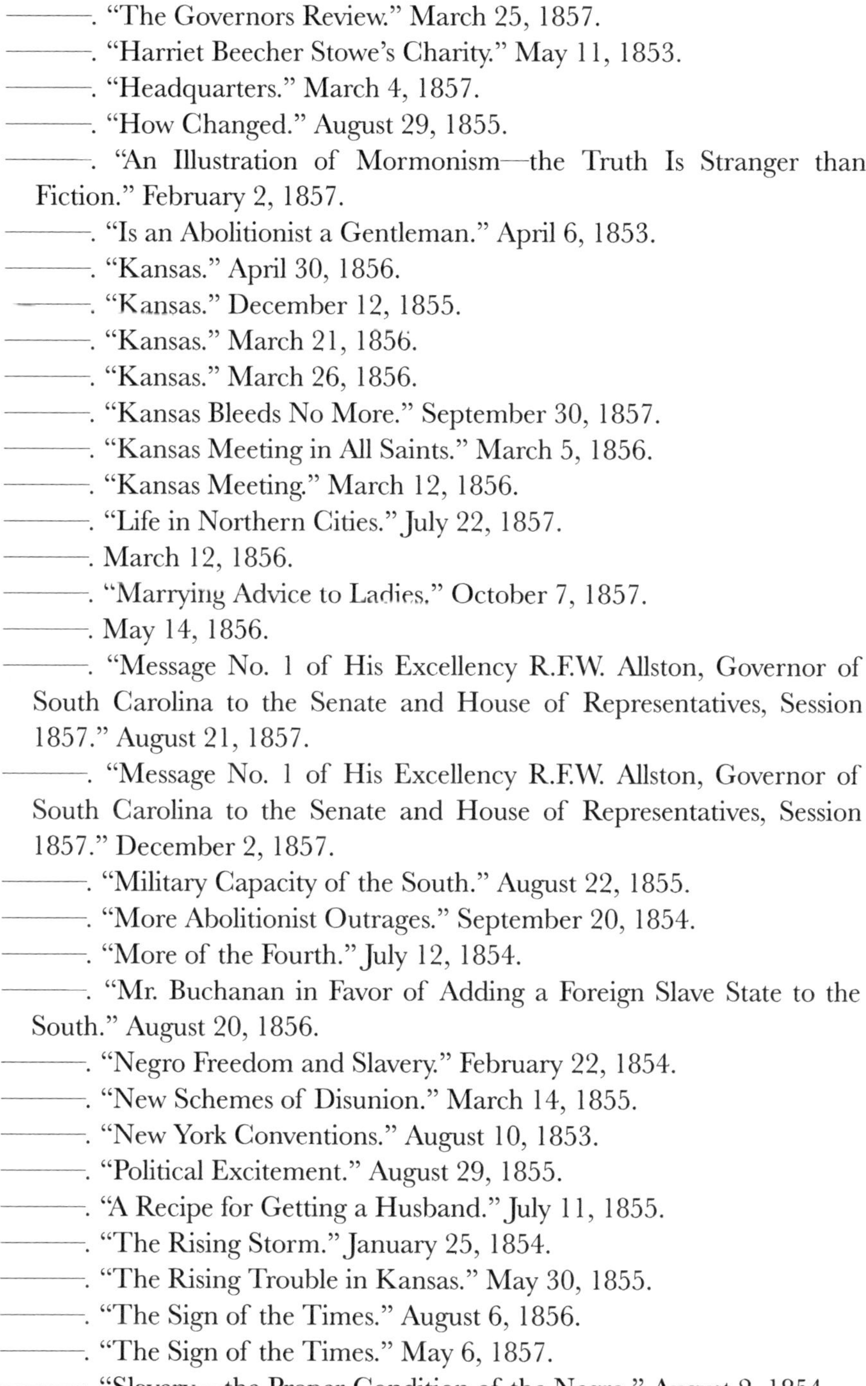

———. "The Governors Review." March 25, 1857.

———. "Harriet Beecher Stowe's Charity." May 11, 1853.

———. "Headquarters." March 4, 1857.

———. "How Changed." August 29, 1855.

———. "An Illustration of Mormonism—the Truth Is Stranger than Fiction." February 2, 1857.

———. "Is an Abolitionist a Gentleman." April 6, 1853.

———. "Kansas." April 30, 1856.

———. "Kansas." December 12, 1855.

———. "Kansas." March 21, 1856.

———. "Kansas." March 26, 1856.

———. "Kansas Bleeds No More." September 30, 1857.

———. "Kansas Meeting in All Saints." March 5, 1856.

———. "Kansas Meeting." March 12, 1856.

———. "Life in Northern Cities." July 22, 1857.

———. March 12, 1856.

———. "Marrying Advice to Ladies." October 7, 1857.

———. May 14, 1856.

———. "Message No. 1 of His Excellency R.F.W. Allston, Governor of South Carolina to the Senate and House of Representatives, Session 1857." August 21, 1857.

———. "Message No. 1 of His Excellency R.F.W. Allston, Governor of South Carolina to the Senate and House of Representatives, Session 1857." December 2, 1857.

———. "Military Capacity of the South." August 22, 1855.

———. "More Abolitionist Outrages." September 20, 1854.

———. "More of the Fourth." July 12, 1854.

———. "Mr. Buchanan in Favor of Adding a Foreign Slave State to the South." August 20, 1856.

———. "Negro Freedom and Slavery." February 22, 1854.

———. "New Schemes of Disunion." March 14, 1855.

———. "New York Conventions." August 10, 1853.

———. "Political Excitement." August 29, 1855.

———. "A Recipe for Getting a Husband." July 11, 1855.

———. "The Rising Storm." January 25, 1854.

———. "The Rising Trouble in Kansas." May 30, 1855.

———. "The Sign of the Times." August 6, 1856.

———. "The Sign of the Times." May 6, 1857.

———. "Slavery—the Proper Condition of the Negro." August 2, 1854.

———. "Southern Commercial Convention in Montgomery." April 21, 1858.
———. "To Kansas Emigrants and All Friends of the South." February 6, 1856.
———. "Trade with the North." September 5, 1855.
———. "What Constitutes a Gentleman." May 14, 1856.
———. "What Makes South Carolina So Great." March 9, 1853.
———. "White Slavery in Massachusetts." September 30, 1857.
———. "Who Were the Slave Traders." November 22, 1854.
———. "Who Were the Slave Traders." November 29, 1854.
———. "A Wife's Devotion: Or the Chivalry of Love." April 18, 1855.
Phillips, Ulrich. *Plantation and Frontier Documents 1649–1863: Illustrative of Industrial History in the Colonial and Ante-bellum South.* Vol. 1. Cleveland, OH: Arthur H. Clark, Company, 1909.
Pringle, Elizabeth Waties Allston. *Chronicles of Chicora Wood.* Charleston, SC: C. Scribner's Sons, 1922.
Reynolds, Emily Bellinger, and Joan Reynolds Faunt. *Biographical Directory of the Senate of South Carolina, 1776–1964.* Columbia: South Carolina Archives Department, 1964.
Rhett, Robert Barnwell. "The Address of the People of South Carolina, Assembled in Convention, to the People of the Slaveholding States of the United States." Charleston, SC: Evans and Cogswell, n.d.
Rogers, George C. *The History of Georgetown County, South Carolina.* Columbia: University of South Carolina Press, 1970.
Selections from Letters and Speeches of the Honorable James H. Hammond. New York: J.F. Trow and Company Printers, 1866.
Silverman, Jason H. "South Carolina." In *A Nation of Sovereign States: Secession and War in the Confederacy.* Edited by Archie P. McDonald. Murfreesboro, TN: Southern Heritage Press, 1994.
South Carolina Department of Archives and History. *Agricultural Survey*, 1850 Census.
———. *Agricultural Survey*, 1860 Census.
South Carolina Historical Magazine 55. "Delegates to the South Carolina Secession Convention of 1860, with a Summary of Date from Manuscript Returns of Schedules 1 and 2 of the United States Census for 1860" (1954): 192–97.
True Republican. "Southern Convention." February 13, 1850.
United States Bureau of Census. *Agricultural Survey of Horry District*, 1850.
———. *South Carolina Industry Schedule*, 1850.

———. *South Carolina Industry Schedule*, 1860.
Washington Union. "Southern State Convention." October 17, 1849.
Weston, Plowden Charles Jennett. *An Address by Plowden C.J. Weston before the Citizens of All Saints Parish at Watchesaw 4th July, 1857*. Georgetown, 1857.
———. *Documents Connected with the History of South Carolina.* London: Cheswick Press, 1856.
Winyah Intelligencer. January 2, 1833.
———. "States' Rights Convention in Charleston." February 8, 1832.
Winyah Observer. "Annexation." May 4, 1844.
———. "Annexation of Canada." February 8, 1845.
———. "The Anniversary of Our National Independence." July 12, 1845.
———. "Anti-Sabbath Convention." March 3, 1848.
———. April 18, 1849.
———. "Australian Cotton." December 8, 1847.
———. "The Battle of King's Mountain; or Hero's Revenge." October 9, 1850.
———. "Book of Mormon." July 14, 1841.
———. "Celebration of the 4th on the Pee Dee." July 13, 1844.
———. "Celebration of the 22nd." February 24, 1844.
———. "Convention of Southern Rights Association." May 14, 1851.
———. "A Day at Lowell." November 11, 1846.
———. December 8, 1847.
———. December 15, 1852.
———. December 1, 1852.
———. "Democratic Party Meeting." April 12, 1848.
———. "Depend Upon Yourself and God Will Lead You." December 14, 1850.
———. "Diffusion of Christianity." November 18, 1844.
———. "District Meeting." April 11, 1849.
———. "Divisions of the South." November 18, 1850.
———. "Domestic Training." November 1, 1848.
———. "The Escape of the Paredes." September 1, 1847.
———. February 7, 1849.
———. "The First Secession of South Carolina." June 11, 1851.
———. "4th of July." July 7, 1851.
———. "4th of July at Johnsonville." July 18, 1849.
———. "Fourth of July Celebration." July 4, 1849.
———. "From New Mexico and the Plains." April 19, 1848.
———. "Gallery of Industry and Enterprise." May 12, 1852.

———. "Georgetown and All Saints Southern Rights Association." October 16, 1850.
———. "Georgetown and All Saints Southern Rights Association." October 23, 1850.
———. "A Good Wife." April 7, 1841.
———. "Head Quarters 8th Brigade, S.C.M." February 27, 1850.
———. "Head Quarters 8th Regiment Cavalry, Order No. 8." May 3, 1848.
———. "Head Quarters of Lower Battalion." February 27, 1850.
———. "Horry Celebration." July 4, 1845.
———. "How to Treat a Wife." July 9, 1851.
———. "In Congress." February 2, 1850.
———. July 7, 1842.
———. July 6, 1844.
———. June 23, 1851.
———. "Martin Van Buren." May 4, 1844.
———. May 8, 1841.
———. May 4, 1844.
———. May 12, 1852.
———. "Military Parade at Black Mingo." December 6, 1843.
———. "Mr. Calhoun's Death." April 3, 1850.
———. "Mr. Calhoun's Speech." March 9, 1850.
———. "Mr. Calhoun's Speech." March 16, 1850.
———. "North and South: Van Buren, Cass, and Taylor: Which Can the South Support?" August 9, 1848.
———. November 18, 1850.
———. November 13, 1850.
———. October 2, 1850.
———. "On Annexation of Canada." July 18, 1849.
———. "The Policy of the South." February 12, 1851.
———. "Proceedings of the Democratic States' Rights Party." May 4, 1841.
———. "Profanity—Don't Do It." March 3, 1847.
———. "Railroad Convention in Memphis." May 12, 1852.
———. "The Repeal of the Corn Laws." March 11, 1846.
———. "The Right of Secession." October 8, 1851.
———. September 9, 1851.
———. "Slavery and the Constitution." May 1, 1850.
———. "The Slavery Question." January 19, 1850.
———. "The Slavery Question and the Missouri Compromise." August 7, 1850.

———. "The Southern Convention at Nashville." June 19, 1850.
———. "Southern Rights Association of All Saints Parish." December 11, 1850.
———. "State of the Poll." September 9, 1845.
———. "A Story of the Cowpens." April 12, 1851.
———. "The Temperance Oath." February 26, 1842.
———. "Washingtonian's Temperance Oath." July 23, 1842.
———. "The Welfare of Our Town." April 10, 1841.
———. "Whig Party Meeting." May 17, 1848.
———. "Who Has Betrayed the South?" July 25, 1849.
———. "Woman: Her Mission and Destiny." November 11, 1844.
———. "Women." November 1, 1848.
———. "The Worth of a Woman." November 20, 1844.

Index

A

B

C

D

E

F

G

Y

About the Author

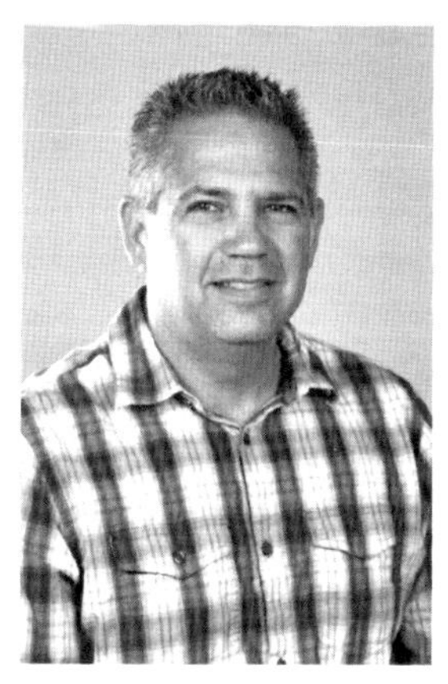

Christopher C. Boyle is a full-time social studies teacher at Socastee High School, Myrtle Beach, South Carolina, and a part-time teaching associate at Coastal Carolina University, Conway, South Carolina. Upon graduation from Coastal Carolina University with his bachelor's degree in history, he further studied history at Winthrop University, where he graduated in 1996 with his Master of Arts degree in American history. He is the author of *Mansfield Plantation: A Legacy on the Black River* and more than a dozen articles on Lowcountry history.